A FEAST FOR ADVENT

By the same author:

A Feast for Lent
A Journey Into God

A FEAST FOR
ADVENT

DELIA SMITH

Text copyright © Delia Smith 1983

The author asserts the moral right
to be identified as the author of this work

Published by
The Bible Reading Fellowship
First Floor, Elsfield Hall
15–17 Elsfield Way
Oxford OX2 8FG

ISBN 978 0 7459 3519 5

First edition 1983 (reprinted three times)
Second edition 1991 (reprinted three times)
Third edition 1994
This edition 1996
10 9 8 7 6

Acknowledgments
Scripture quotations taken from The Jerusalem Bible © 1966 by Darton, Longman & Todd Ltd and
Doubleday & Company Inc.

Scripture quotations from The Revised Standard Version of the Bible, copyright © 1946, 1952, 1971
by the Division of Christian Education of the National Council of the Churches of Christ in the
United States of America, are used by permission. All rights reserved.

The Psalms: a new translation © 1963 The Grail (England). Verse references follow those in the Bible,
while the numbering in the Grail version is indicated by the figures in square brackets.

Quotation on page 124 taken from *Hallowing the Time* by Geoffrey Preston, published and
copyrighted © 1980 by Darton, Longman & Todd (in USA: Paulist Press), and used by permission
of the publishers.

A catalogue record for this book is available from the British Library

Printed in Singapore by Craft Print International Ltd

Keep the word of God, for 'blessed are they who keep it'. Let it pierce deep into your inmost soul and penetrate your feelings and actions. Eat well and your soul will delight and grow. Do not forget to eat your bread or your heart will wither, but let your soul feast richly. If you keep the word of God in this way, without a doubt you will be kept by it.

St Bernard of Clairvaux (1090–1153)

CONTENTS

FOREWORDS

We all have favourite passages from scripture. Three of mine are about the Word of God itself. The writer of Hebrews calls the Word of God 'something alive and active' (4:12). The prophet Isaiah reminds us that the Word of God will not return to him empty handed but will succeed 'in what it was sent to do' (55:11). And then there is the exasperated comment from the man reading the scriptures in his chariot; Philip heard him reading aloud and asked him if he understood what he was reading. 'How can I' he exclaimed, 'unless I have someone to guide me?' (Acts 8:31).

There are so many today who share that man's desire and exasperation. It is one of Delia Smith's gifts to be able to guide those who like him are searching the scriptures, and to lead them to prayer. Like every good guide she has an infectious enthusiasm (which is faith and love) for her task. You can be sure that if you walk with her on this particular pilgrimage the Word of God will do its work in you in one way or another, and that you will discover something of its refreshing liveliness and activity.

Advent can be an exciting time. It is a good time to come afresh—or even for the first time—to God's Word, because it is a time of new beginnings. With Isaiah and Mary and all creation we wait expectantly for a birth. Every birthday is a time of wonder and hope, but surrounding this birthday is a simply breath-catching expectancy, for it celebrates the birth of God's Son, the Word made Flesh. Delia Smith's faithful journey through Advent touches the season beautifully. It is hopeful, full of love and trust, and encouraging to all those who wish, like her, to break the bread of God's Word and share it with others.

I am delighted to have been asked to recommend these lovely Advent reflections. May those who read them enjoy to the full a well-prepared and beautifully balanced feast.

David Konstant

Bishop of Leeds

Advent? Mmm... Lent, now—that's when you do without sweets or take saccharin instead of sugar, if you're that way inclined of course. But Advent—well, I don't really know.

I suspect that, if we're honest, most of us come into the 'don't know' category where Advent is concerned. The shops piously offer us Advent calendars once the summer holidays are over, so it must be something to do with Christmas. When my own children opened the twenty-five little cardboard doors of their calendar every day in December, I used to feel mild outrage at the robins, teddy bears, dolls and Santas thereby revealed. But my own build-up to Christmas was scarcely less secular. December days were for puddings, pies and presents, a madly accelerating dash towards the big blow-out on Christmas Day. With, of course, a statutory nod in the direction of the Christ child in his crib on Christmas morning. Very cosy.

Delia Smith has ensured that from now on things will be different. It goes without saying that in her case the puddings and pies will be superlatively well attended to; but in this book, with all the simplicity which is her hall-mark, she points to the deep, underlying significance of the weeks leading up to Christmas. In those four weeks we wait for, hope for, prepare for the coming of the promised Messiah. It is a period of 'starters' in preparation for the splendid 'main course'. Delia provides us with the brief daily meditations and reflections which will sharpen our appetite and longing for the events of Christmas, but which will also provide a satisfaction all their own. In Advent the cry goes out for us to wake up, to get rid of our absurd complacency and self-regard and to gird ourselves for the challenge posed by the advent of Christ. In helping us to understand the true meaning of Advent, Delia Smith has made it possible for us to experience the real joy of Christmas.

Mary Craig   **Writer and broadcaster**

INTRODUCTION

When I look back at my introduction to the first edition of the book in 1983, I can't help a wry smile. *A Feast for Advent* was intended to help me, and others, to make contemplation of the coming of God into the world central to those four weeks leading up to Christmas. If—ran the sentiments in that original introduction—we find time for prayer and contemplation, we will not be too exhausted to celebrate 'the greatest birth in the history of mankind'.

Well, we can all dream! Eleven years later, and eleven years wiser, I have come closer to understanding the truth, which is that prayer and contemplation, while utterly necessary, do absolutely nothing to ease the pressure and that on Christmas Day I will always end up horizontal! Since the first edition was published I have had the privilege not only of preparing the feast for my family and friends, but also of sharing that organisation and preparation on television with millions of others. If there's going to be a feast, there's always going to have to be someone to prepare it.

Nevertheless I would still like to introduce the following pages as a help for others who, like myself, find themselves battered and pressured by Christmas preparations, to escape for a few moments each day and try to find some space for God. Even if your limbs are aching and your head is spinning with trying to remember everything, even if you nod off while you're reading, don't be afraid to be human. The *intention* is what counts, or as St Teresa of Avila once said: 'It's not with many thoughts or words that He hears us but in the silence of our longing...'

Happy Christmas

Delia Smith   **1994**

Awakening to God

Christians awake!

◆◆

You know 'the time' has come: you must wake up now: our salvation is even nearer than it was when we were converted. The night is almost over, it will be daylight soon—let us give up all the things we prefer to do under cover of the dark; let us arm ourselves and appear in the light.

(Romans 13:11—12)

On the first Sunday of Advent a cry goes out to the people of God. Not a gentle, coaxing appeal but a loud and dramatic exhortation. Wake up! The time has come! As we enter the period of preparation for celebrating the coming of God as Man, we are urged to be attentive to the present age which his birth has established. This is the 'time' of Jesus in which the gospel message is preached to all nations, a time when the secret thoughts of men's hearts will be revealed. It is a time of judgement or—more specifically—of testing when, if we are awake to the work of the Holy Spirit within us, we shall be ready for the final glorious coming of God when his kingdom will finally be established.

St Paul has taken up a theme that recurs in the Bible, that of being 'awake'; like the bride in the canticles who sleeps while her heart is awake. The awakened heart is the heart of one who is spiritually alert to the continuing presence of God: 'I hear my Beloved knocking' (Song of Songs 5:2). It's the heart that listens to the still small voice of the Holy Spirit within, and responds.

In both the Old and New Testaments this vigilant faith is illustrated by what the Bible calls 'the watch'. The watchman forgoes his sleep to keep guard and prevent enemies invading under the cover of darkness. It is from simple images like this in the Bible that we can draw out so much helpful teaching: if we are not watchful we can be lulled into a kind of spiritual complacency—which presents the ideal conditions for the very subtle assault of the enemy. He will be delighted to entice us into a settled, cosy routine of worship, prayer and good works so that we become too preoccupied to be attentive to the fresh challenges that God relentlessly calls us to.

Someone who strives to be spiritually awake is not only watching for the enemy, he is watching also for God, looking out for him, listening for his voice. 'I hear my Beloved. See how he comes... My Beloved lifts up his voice, he says to me, "Come"' (Song of Songs 2:8, 10). Through the prophet Isaiah, too, we hear how we must watch for the coming of God: 'On your walls, Jerusalem, I set watchmen. Day or night they must never be silent. You who keep the Lord mindful *must take no rest*. Nor let him take rest till he has restored Jerusalem' (Isaiah 62:6–7). And Jesus himself echoes the idea when he exhorts his disciples to 'stay awake' and continually 'watch and pray' (Matthew 24–26).

Today we begin to anticipate the joyful experience of the birth of Jesus. But in order to prepare for it we must pray for new birth within ourselves, pray that God will do something new in our lives and awaken us from our complacent sleep. We live in a secular world shrouded in the darkness of unbelief, but we have accepted the light that enlightens all men (John 1:9) and we must allow it to penetrate our darkness, to heal and restore us so that we in turn can become a light in the world. When someone has a deep prayer life and is learning to move into more profound belief, repentance and more radical commitment, the grace of God in their lives can flow out very powerfully to others.

PRAYER

My soul is waiting for the Lord,
I count on his word.
My soul is longing for the Lord
more than watchman for daybreak...
Because with the Lord there is mercy
and fullness of redemption

(Psalm 130[129]:5–7)

MEDITATION
Read Matthew 24:37–44

Come, let us go up to the mountain of the Lord

◆◆

In the days to come
the mountain of the Temple of the Lord
shall tower above the mountains
and be lifted higher than the hills.
All the nations will stream to it,
peoples without number will come to it;
and they will say:
'Come, let us go up to the mountain of the Lord,
to the Temple of the God of Jacob
that he may teach us his ways
so that we may walk in his paths;
since the Law will go out from Zion,
and the oracle of the Lord from Jerusalem'.

(Isaiah 2:2–3)

Advent, with all its appropriate texts and readings, is a time to look back at the story of God's people, to reflect on the roots of our faith and the unfolding history of our salvation. Myself, I never cease to wonder at the enormously long tradition which has formed the Christian faith. In Britain we are considered to be staunch traditionalists who take tremendous pride in our heritage, yet it seems so small when we compare it with the Christian tradition stretching right back to Abraham.

On a visit to the Holy Land it struck me that while the archaeologists uncover layer upon layer of countless civilisations, the Christian (or Jewish) pilgrim can simply visit a place called Mamre at Hebron—where Abraham pitched his tent and built an altar to the Lord (Genesis 13:18)—and there reflect on how the tradition took root, and was recorded and kept alive by the writers and editors of holy scripture, thus passing on the message of eternal life through the ages to the present day. There is so much inspiration we can draw from this story of a people who, though not living in the messianic age of full revelation, kept alive their faith in the one true God against all the odds.

Over the next four weeks we shall be hearing quite a lot from one of these people, a man who is described as the greatest of all the prophets who proclaimed the coming of a messiah, Isaiah. He lived in an age of great insecurity and turmoil, an age of a thousand gods when every nation and every part of creation had its own. But, a faithful son of David, Isaiah had a vision while visiting the Temple one day: in his vision he grasps, with awe, the transcendent holiness of the one almighty universal God, whose glory fills the whole earth (Isaiah 6). He also comprehends, in contrast, the utter poverty of sinful human nature. 'What a wretched state I am in! I am lost, for I am a man of unclean lips and I live among a people of unclean lips, and my eyes have looked at the King, Yahweh Sabaoth!'

But Isaiah's lips are purified, and he volunteers to proclaim his belief to the people—even though he is warned that their hearts will be closed to his message. Now that Isaiah has understood the almightiness of God and the frailty of the people, he totally trusts in God's providence. When news reaches the people that two invading armies have joined forces in order to confront Jerusalem, the hearts of the king and the people are gripped with fear. But Isaiah is reassuring: 'Do not fear' he tells them, 'keep calm, do not let your heart sink...'—but he goes on to warn the king: 'If you will not *believe*, surely you shall not be established' (ch. 7). Here is the very core of Isaiah's message, echoed so resoundingly in chapter 43: 'I, I am the Lord your God, there is no other saviour but me'.

Isaiah's belief enabled him to speak of things he could not possibly have understood in human terms. In the text for today he is foretelling something that must have seemed extraordinarily unlikely—that *all* nations would worship the God of his ancestors. Yet two and a half millennia later we are witnesses to that fact; the good news Isaiah prophesied has now reached all nations and 'peoples without number' embrace the Christian faith and worship the one true God, the God of Jacob.

One of the first Gentile converts in the New Testament was the Roman centurion, fulfilling Isaiah's prophecy about 'all nations'. He was a man whose belief in Jesus was so pure and simple that he was able to say, with all the odds stacked against him, 'only say the word, and my servant will be healed' (Matthew 8:8). The Gospel tells us that Jesus was astonished at his faith and said, 'You have believed, so let this be done'. As we pray for a new awakening to the truth, let us also pray for the courage to believe and that our belief may become—like that of Isaiah and the centurion—a living reality of trust and self-abandonment, however difficult the circumstances.

PRAYER

Almighty God, let me share in the vision of your glory,
though I am unworthy to receive. Help me to believe
that your saving power can enter every area of my life,
and through the spoken word receive your healing touch.
I ask this through Jesus our Lord in the power of your
Holy Spirit.
Amen

MEDITATION
Read Matthew 8:5–11

The message of peace

◆◆

The wolf lives with the lamb,
the panther lies down with the kid,
calf and lion cub feed together
with a little boy to lead them.
The cow and the bear make friends,
their young lie down together.
The lion eats straw like the ox.
The infant plays over the cobra's hole;
into the viper's lair
the young child puts his hand.
They do no hurt, no harm,
on all my holy mountain,
for the earth is filled
with the knowledge of the Lord
as the waters swell the sea.

(Isaiah 11:6–9)

One of the miracles of prophecy—which continues to fascinate me—is the many layers of interpretation which can be put on the proclamations of the prophets. Part of Isaiah's prophecy would happen within his own lifetime or in the foreseeable future. Part of it (as we discussed yesterday) could only be understood after the birth, death and resurrection of Jesus. And part of it, even now 2,000 years after those events, is still about the future.

The passage above is as yet quite beyond our present range of experience, yet it points to our ultimate hope as believers when God's kingdom will finally be established ('when the earth is filled with the knowledge of the Lord') and all of creation will be reconciled in total peace.

One of the very first images that Isaiah imparts in his prophecy is the image of mother and child. In all the political turmoil of his time he is given this picture which transcends generations and illustrates so effectively the image of peace. It is a picture that has been painted and sculpted by artists in every age, and today we have only to look at nature and see any mother and her tiny baby to understand that the peace and harmony between the two is precisely the relationship to which God and his creation will ultimately be restored. Thus the creative word of God is written in nature as well as in scripture.

Really to appreciate the above reading I think we need to reflect back to the third chapter of Genesis (vv. 14–16) wherein war is declared between creation and its enemy, between woman and the serpent: 'I will make you enemies of each other, you and the woman, her offspring and your offspring'. Yet even within this chilling text are the seeds of total victory—for a descendant of the woman will eventually crush the head of the serpent! The drama of life begins with a woman and her offspring; Isaiah signals the Messiah with the image of mother and child; and finally in the Book of Revelation we find the symbolism of a woman crowned with stars who gives birth to a male child who ultimately triumphs over the dragon (Satan).

With the passage above, Isaiah takes us beyond the final battle, drawing for us a picture of established peace when all of nature lives in harmony; and death, pain, violence and anger are no more. Notice, three times we are given the image of a child, which to me shows so clearly God's ultimate plan and his desire to be a mother and father, and we the little children for whom he provides and cares.

As we pray for growth in belief, we will learn to trust. Trust is the yardstick which measures belief. Our goal is a simple, childlike trust in God in every area of our lives. St Paul's 'weakness' was his simplicity and trust, which enabled God to work so powerfully in his life. 'When I am weak, then I am strong' (2 Corinthians 12:10). Jesus, when he saw the disciples respond to this, cried out with all the joy of the spirit: 'I bless you, Father, Lord of heaven and earth, for hiding these things from the learned and the clever, and revealing them to mere children' (Luke 10:21).

PRAYER

O Lord, my heart is not proud,
nor haughty my eyes.
I have not gone after things too great
nor marvels beyond me.
Truly I have set my soul
in silence and peace.
A weaned child on its mother's breast,
even so is my soul.

(Psalm 131[130]:1–2)

MEDITATION
Read Luke 10:21–24

The healing banquet ADVENT 1/WEDNESDAY

◆◆◆

On this mountain,
the Lord of hosts will prepare for all peoples
a banquet of rich food, a banquet of fine wines,
of food rich and juicy, of fine strained wines.
On this mountain he will remove
the mourning veil covering all peoples,
and the shroud enwrapping all nations,
he will destroy Death for ever.
The Lord God will wipe away
the tears from every cheek;
he will take away his people's shame
everywhere on earth,
for the Lord has said so.
That day, it will be said: See, this is our God
in whom we hoped for salvation;
the Lord is the one in whom we hoped.
We exult and we rejoice
that he has saved us;
for the hand of the Lord
rests on this mountain.

(Isaiah 25:6–10)

Ｏne of the most stimulating aspects of scripture study is the way in which it begins, as we search the Old Testament, to open out and become a commentary on the New. It is almost as if the Old Testament is underlining the New, dotting the 'i's and crossing the 't's, giving us a greater depth of vision. Jesus himself, when he joins the confused disciples on the road to Emmaus, explains the scriptures to them: 'starting with Moses and going through all the prophets' he expounds to them the passages that were about himself! The disciples, in fact, only recognise him when he sits at their table and blesses and breaks bread, but after that he refers to the scriptures again: 'Everything written about me in the Law of Moses, in the Prophets and the Psalms has to be fulfilled' (Luke 24:27, 44).

It's in this context that today we can reflect on the theme of food and the Bible's imagery of feasting and banquets. From the very beginning a shared meal symbolises a sacred bond between those who share it, both with each other and with God. In Genesis (ch. 14), when Abraham meets the king and high priest Melchizedek and offers him one-tenth of his possessions, they share bread and wine as a sacred sign of their unity. Thus even that far back our own eucharistic celebration is foreshadowed. This theme of Christian worship becomes central as the story of the people of God unfolds: the people partake in the communal sacrifice of the lamb to atone for their sins; the passover lamb is eaten before the exodus takes place; and during it they were fed on bread from heaven (which not only sustained them on their journey, but was also symbolic of the presence of God among them—so much so that God commanded Moses to place a jar filled with manna inside the ark of the covenant next to the tables of the Law).

So we see that both the written word of God and the heavenly bread symbolised God's presence among his people as far back as the Exodus. Today we are still a people of the book and the bread, and our worship of God is still centred on these two. This theme of 'spiritual food' can provide us with hours of reflection—especially if we compare the reading above with the events recorded in Matthew 15.

What Isaiah sees as a vision, St Matthew reports as a reality in the feeding of the multitude. In the vision the people come to a mountain and meet God, who will heal them of darkness and pain and save them from death. 'See, this is our God in whom we hoped for salvation.' In Matthew we find Jesus going up into the mountains of Galilee to preach, the crowds gathering and there receiving healing. Through Jesus the 'mourning veil' is lifted: the blind see, the deaf hear, the lame walk, their shame is taken away, their tears are wiped away, the dumb begin to speak and 'exult and rejoice' in the saving power of the Lord. But that's not all. The Lord provides a banquet—so much food that the people 'all ate as much as they wanted' and there was still plenty left over.

What we must glean from these two readings—and pray for—is spiritual healing in our own lives, that our eyes and ears may be opened to see and hear everything God wants to communicate to each of us individually. If we suffer from lameness in our walk with God, if we're not able to make the journey, we must pray for strength. To gain that strength we must be partakers at the banquet, feeding on the word of God daily, coming with the crowds to sit at the feet of Jesus, listening to his words, allowing them to heal and transform us.

Remember that, in the physical sense, those who go without food for any length of time lose the desire to eat. ('Do not forget to eat or your soul will wither': Bernard of Clairvaux.) Let us learn how to recognise that deep hunger that only God can satisfy. 'I am the bread of life. He who comes to me will never be hungry; he who believes in me will never thirst' (John 6:35). Jesus' final instruction, repeated three times in a kind of impassioned plea, was 'feed my sheep, feed my lambs'. And above all, there was the great promise of the beatitudes: 'Blessed are those who hunger and thirst for righteousness, for *they shall be satisfied*' (Matthew 5:6).

PRAYER

You have prepared a banquet for me
in the sight of my foes.
My head you have anointed with oil;
my cup is overflowing.
Surely goodness and kindness shall follow me
all the days of my life.
In the Lord's own house shall I dwell
for ever and ever.

(Psalm 23[22]:5–6)

MEDITATION
Read Matthew 15:29–37

The safety of the rock

◆◆

'Therefore, everyone who listens to these words of mine and acts on them will be like a sensible man who built his house on rock. Rain came down, floods rose, gales blew and hurled themselves against that house, and it did not fall: it was founded on rock. But everyone who listens to these words of mine and does not act on them will be like a stupid man who built his house on sand. Rain came down, floods rose, gales blew and struck that house, and it fell; and what a fall it had!'

(Matthew 7:24–27)

Today's reading takes us a stage further on from yesterday's. Simply hearing the word of God is not enough. Being willing to listen is the first requirement, but being willing to act and be obedient to what the word is saying—that is the acid test. If we're really committed to hearing the word of God, one of the things it will begin to teach us is the ultimate test of our belief: trust in God's providence in all the circumstances of our lives.

First, though, let's look at yet another of the portraits in the Bible of what God is like. This time we are given the image of the rock, symbolising strength, safety, total security. It was also an image the prophet Isaiah perceived when he proclaimed that we should 'trust in the Lord for ever, for the Lord is the everlasting Rock' (26:4). His strength, in other words, is eternal, invulnerable to storms or other hazards: his faithfulness and mercy last from age to age. But equally powerful is the image of refuge and safety—as the psalmist asserts: 'Be a rock of refuge for me, a mighty stronghold to save me' (31[30]:2). In the shifting landscape of the desert, the rock as a symbol of permanence is a very comprehensible one for people to grasp.

In the course of the exodus the rock becomes providential. When Moses strikes it with his staff, it provides water in the desert—and St Paul explains (1 Corinthians 10:4) that this rock was Christ, through whom the Holy Spirit would be poured out as living water to bless all mankind. When Jesus gives Simon a new name, it is Cephas (Peter) meaning 'rock'. He promises that his Church will be steadfast, eternal.

So we are instructed to build our faith on an everlasting rock. A belief that will endure suffering and hardship is one that is based on solid reality, and if we are obedient to the word of God we will eventually begin to step out in trust, understanding that this rock-like power can sustain us far beyond anything we can imagine. But to say 'Lord, Lord', to do all the right things, even to offer a lifetime of good works, is not enough. What the gospel teaches us is radical commitment and radical trust: Jesus himself tells us, 'Do not worry about anything, set your hearts on the kingdom of heaven and God's righteousness *first*, and all that you need will be given to you as well' (end of Matthew 6).

I believe one of the signs of a life lived in obedience to the word of God is serenity. Serenity in a person is a sure sign of faith built on a rock of trust. And to achieve this we need to *build up* a relationship of real trust by learning how to trust God in the little, everyday circumstances of our lives. If you are a person who tends to worry, why not start right now? Just pray and ask the Holy Spirit to bring to mind some small anxiety that has been nagging away at you, then simply ask God to deal with it. Every time you feel it coming back to niggle, you just say a very short prayer: 'Into your hands, Lord, I commend such and such'. Then when you see how simply and easily God deals with it, offer thanks and take another step of trust.

The spiritual journey of trust can be very stimulating and exciting, but we can only learn to trust in big things if we start with the small. If you look at a map of the Middle East you'll see that 40 years to make the exodus from Egypt was a long time to make such a short journey: but that was because God was training the people to trust—and every time they failed he sent them off on another lap! In more modern terms, if you want to move more quickly on your journey with the Lord, remember: the fast lane on the motorway is called trust.

PRAYER

In God is my safety and glory,
the rock of my strength.
Take refuge in God all you people.
Trust him at all times.
Pour out your hearts before him
for God is our refuge.

(Psalm 62[61]:7–8)

MEDITATION
Read Isaiah 26:1–6

Do you believe?   ADVENT 1/FRIDAY
◆◆◆

As Jesus went on his way two blind men followed him shouting,
'Take pity on us, Son of David'. And when Jesus reached the
house the blind men came up with him and he said to them, 'Do
you believe I can do this?' They said, 'Sir, we do'. Then he
touched their eyes saying, 'Your faith deserves it, so let this be done
for you'. And their sight returned. Then Jesus sternly warned
them, 'Take care that no one learns about this'. But when they
had gone, they talked about him all over the countryside.

(Matthew 9:27–31)

As we progress through the readings for Advent, what we find the Bible is giving us is a series of pictures flashed onto the screens of our minds showing us the coming of the Messiah, first through the eyes of the prophets, and then through the actual experiences of the four evangelists.

Isaiah gives us many glimpses not only of what the 'Holy One' will be like, but of how the people will respond to him. 'They will hallow the Holy One of Jacob, stand in awe of the God of Israel... the lowly will rejoice... erring spirits will learn wisdom' (29:23–24, 19). But surely one of the most extraordinary signs is the often-repeated proclamation of the Messiah's miraculous healing powers. 'The deaf that day will hear the words of a book and, after shadow and darkness, the eyes of the blind will see' (29:18). Well, perhaps in the light of the Gospels it doesn't seem so extraordinary for us, but for the prophet this really was something very new.

It is true that throughout the history of Israel God had often revealed his love for his people and his saving power by signs and wonders. For Noah the great sign of the covenant was the rainbow that circled the earth. We can recall the plagues of Egypt, the parting of the Red Sea, the sun standing still for Joshua, the walls of Jericho tumbling down. But what we see in these are signs of God's power, which while illustrating his greatness are reversals of the natural order, demonstrations of things quite outside normal human experience.

But when the messianic kingdom is established in the person of Jesus, the signs and wonders take on an altogether new meaning: 'Behold, I make all things new' says the Book of Revelation. With the birth of Jesus the work of the new creation, the new heaven and the new earth are being established, and the signs and wonders are now taking place *within* the natural order. All the miracles of Jesus are works of restoration, healing and wholeness. In the building of the kingdom the people will be able to 'restore ruined cities' and 'raise what has long lain waste' (Isaiah 61:4). So while Jesus himself is the 'sign' of the beginning of the new creation, his healing miracles are the signs that he is indeed the Holy One proclaimed by the prophets.

Before reflecting on the particular miracle in our reading, there's one important point that needs to be made. While all Jesus' miracles are real in the physical sense, they also always have a deeper spiritual significance—and it is this underlying meaning that provides food for prayer and contemplation. In the Bible blindness represents unbelief. Later on in Advent we shall be considering *the* underlying theme of Bible teaching—that is, darkness and light representing death or life. But here we see two people having a problem with their unbelief yet willing to do something about it. They're not happy in their unbelief, so they make a decision to follow Jesus even though at that moment they cannot see him. The narrative doesn't say how long the journey was, though the other version (Matthew 20:29–34) suggests it was from Jericho to Jerusalem, which is a sizeable trek even if you are not blind. But these blind men sound persistent and willing to persevere with heartfelt prayer.

It seems to me, from the manner in which they addressed him, that they believed at that point that Jesus was the Messiah ('Son of David' is the title of the Messiah recalled by Nathan's prophecy to David in 2 Samuel 7: 'Your House and your sovereignty will always stand secure before me and your throne be established for ever'). Jesus responds by asking them a question: 'Do you believe I can do this?' and the answer seems to come from the heart. 'Sir, we do' and they are healed.

What we need to draw from this, as we grapple with unbelief in our own lives, is the necessity to *keep on* following Jesus, to be persistent in prayer, earnestly to desire to receive more and more sight as we learn to step out in faith. So, as we receive more healing, so will the shadows recede and our vision become sharpened. The more we begin to see him, the more he will awaken in us the reality of his work of restoration and healing within us. 'Happy are those who have not seen and yet believe' (John 20:29).

PRAYER

He is happy who is helped by Jacob's God,
whose hope is in the Lord his God...
the Lord who gives sight to the blind,
who raises up those who are bowed down.

Psalm 146[145]:5, 8)

MEDITATION
Read Isaiah 29:17–24

This is the way, follow it ADVENT 1/SATURDAY

◆◆◆

*He will be gracious to you when he hears you cry; when he hears
he will answer. When the Lord has given you the bread of
suffering and the water of distress, he who is your teacher will
hide no longer, and you will see your teacher with your own eyes.
Whether you turn to right or left, your ears will hear these words
behind you, 'This is the way, follow it'.*

(Isaiah 30:19–21)

The more I search through the Old Testament, the more it seems to me that
a quite definite pattern of teaching emerges, providing us with clear and simple
directions. Briefly it goes like this. If the people (nations as well as individuals)
enter into a relationship with God and trust in his saving power, they will live in
peace and security and he will provide. If they rebel and begin to trust in their
own achievements and ingenuity, inevitably disaster befalls them. When that
disaster occurs, they begin to understand their need for God, they experience a
change of heart and cry out to God to rescue them. God hears their cry,
consoles, comforts and restores them. It's this cyclic pattern of history that
shapes and forms the relationship between God and man. Put in even simpler
terms, trust equals peace and security, rebellion equals judgement and exile,
repentance equals healing and restoration.

There is a tendency, I think, in the modern church to make light of God's
judgement—but if we do that, I believe we then underestimate the more
positive aspects that emerge from a period of judgement or exile. Consider, for
instance, the background to the reading above. In Isaiah's time the tribe of Judah
and the city of Jerusalem were constantly under threat from foreign invaders.
Led by false prophets, the people refuse to trust in God's providence and try to
enter into an alliance with Egypt, imagining that this was their best hope of
security.

In effect the people are putting their trust in a pagan nation who worship
false gods. The true prophet, Isaiah, warns them quite unequivocally: 'For thus
says the Lord your God: your salvation lay in conversion and tranquillity, your
strength in complete trust; and you would have none of it!' (Isaiah 30:15). Not
surprisingly the end result is defeat and a long period of exile in Babylon. *But* the
exile turns out to be a preparation through suffering, and a purification for

future restoration at the coming of the Messiah.

Both on a collective and a personal level, there is much in this simple teaching that we can relate to our own situation today. Chapter 30 of Isaiah can offer much inspiration to pray for world disarmament and understanding of the ultimate futility of any sort of security provided by nuclear alliances and man-made defences. Our stubbornness on these issues could well be a disaster-course to judgement. On a more personal level perhaps we can begin to appreciate some of the more profound and positive effects of suffering. There are many people who have only really been able to discover the possibility of there actually being a God at all through the experience of suffering—when a house built on sand crumbles, the builder is forced to rebuild on more solid foundations. As C.S. Lewis put it: 'God whispers in our pleasure, but shouts in our pain'.

Here, too, I am reminded of the story of the rebellious little lamb who refused pointblank to heed the voice of the shepherd and boldly walked out of the sheepfold into the wild country of thieves, wolves and dangerous ravines. After innumerable attempts to call the lamb by name and make him hear, and after several dangerous rescue operations, the shepherd was finally driven—because of his deep love for the lamb—to break one of its legs, a desperate measure to save the lamb's life. While the leg was broken, the shepherd tended it, bathed it and bound it up, carrying the lamb on his shoulders to console and comfort it. But while this was happening the lamb began to understand how to hear the shepherd's voice, to follow him and thus avoid the dangers that lurked outside. By the time the leg was healed, so was the lamb, understanding that the only way to be safe was to stay close to the shepherd. In Isaiah's message God is just such a person whom the people can hear, see and learn from: a teacher who will point out the way. Though rebellion will bring distress and suffering, there *will* be consolation, healing and restoration.

As we prepare to celebrate the coming of the one true shepherd, let us pray for a new awakening to his presence within each one of us; let us learn to see him, recognise his voice, and listen to it. Jesus is 'the way, the truth and the life' (John 14:6), he is the one true shepherd who calls us *by name* one by one. 'This is the way, follow it.'

PRAYER

Praise the Lord for he is good;
sing to our God for he is loving:
to him our praise is due.
The Lord builds up Jerusalem
and brings back Israel's exiles,
he heals the broken-hearted,
he binds up all their wounds.
He fixes the number of the stars;
he calls each one by its name.

(Psalm 147[146]:1–4)

MEDITATION
Read Matthew 9:35–end

Prepare the Way

The way of the Spirit ADVENT 2

◆◆◆

A shoot springs from the stock of Jesse,
a scion thrusts from his roots.
On him the spirit of the Lord rests,
a spirit of wisdom and insight,
a spirit of counsel and power,
a spirit of knowledge and of the fear of the Lord.
(the fear of the Lord is his breath.)

(Isaiah 11:1–2)

In due course John the Baptist appeared; he preached in the
wilderness of Judaea and this was his message: 'Repent, for the
kingdom of heaven is close at hand'. This was the man the
prophet Isaiah spoke of when he said: 'A voice cries in the
wilderness: Prepare a way for the Lord...'

[John said] 'I baptise you in water for repentance but the one
who follows me is more powerful than I am, and I am not fit to
carry his sandals; he will baptise you with the Holy Spirit and
fire'.

(Matthew 3:1–3, 11)

The themes underlying today's readings are rich and full of meaning, but on
the surface—if we read the full text of Matthew 3:1–12—what we encounter
are crowds of people coming forward to make a renewed commitment to God,

to submit to a ritual cleansing which entails a whole programme of renewal of life. What John is proclaiming is a time of preparation for a new birth.

Let's try for a moment to enter into the scene in the wilderness. Let us try to imagine, if we can, a weary people whose religion must have sunk to a desperately low point. Long gone were the great patriarchs and prophets and with them the great signs and wonders of their past history. Now they lived under pagan occupying forces, with a corrupt king and religious leaders who were both hypocritical and unreal. Yet throughout the history of the people of God there had always been a remnant who remained faithful, who did not lose hope that one day the Messiah would come.

The prophet Malachi's book ends with a prophecy that the great Elijah would return. Thus the Old Testament concludes with a promise which is fulfilled a few pages later at the beginning of the New—because as Jesus explains to his disciples (Matthew 11:14) John the Baptist is 'the Elijah who was to return'. But to get back to the scene on the banks of the Jordan, I feel there is something we can learn from the people who were gathered there. *They* were the people of hope, people who understood their weakness, their need for God and for a renewed relationship with him. They were people—perhaps like us—who found no satisfaction in a world of materialism and hypocrisy. Just as their world was 'occupied' by the forces of secularism and unbelief, so is ours today.

But we, too, must be a people of hope. Though we may be tired, dejected, far away from God, the exhortation still rings out through the centuries to speak directly to us here and now: make way for the Lord, make repentance a reality, be cleansed and purified. If we're like the Pharisees we can go through the motions—church on Sundays, prayer and good works—but unless we are being challenged to grow in faith, our repentance is not 'bearing the appropriate fruit'. What the Baptist summons us to is total commitment, and a renewal of the whole of life which goes far beyond the limitations of this world.

I'm sure it was the *reality* of John the Baptist that attracted those people gathered there: a true witness to God's presence in the world. All of us have the capacity to discern a true witness, and when we find someone who is really communicating life, we are drawn out of our darkness like moths to a flame. But John is not the light itself; all he can do is point to the light, to Jesus. 'Behold, the lamb of God. Behold him who takes away the sins of the world.' Those of us who are willing to start the journey out of darkness, and allow the lamb of God to free us from the sins that separate us from God, will in turn (as we grow in faith) become witnesses to the light.

John was the first great witness, and we are called to be like him, to make the challenge of faith that will shine out and give hope to others. But how can this be? How can a helpless creature like me possibly give life to others? Jesus says of John, 'Of all the children born of women, a greater than John the Baptist has never been seen; yet the least in the kingdom of heaven is greater than he is' (Matthew 11:11).

The answer, then, is the Holy Spirit. By ourselves we can do nothing; we are like Ezekiel's dry bones, wasted and lifeless (ch. 37). On Jesus 'the Spirit of the Lord rests', and if we follow him and receive the Spirit to dwell within us, then it is as if God has breathed on those dry bones ('… they came to life again and stood up on their feet, a great, an immense army'). If we are witnesses that is how the work of the Spirit will take flesh in our lives, raising us up to be part of an immense army.

Today we must pray for this renewing action of the Holy Spirit in each of our lives, so that we might share his gifts of wisdom, insight, counsel, power and knowledge of God. Remember the promise of Jesus: 'I shall ask the Father, and he will give you another Advocate to be with you for ever, that Spirit of truth whom the world can never receive since it neither sees nor knows him; but you know him, because he is with you, he is in you' (John 14:16–17).

PRAYER

Come Holy Spirit, fill the hearts of your faithful,
enkindle in them the fire of your love;
send forth your Spirit, O Lord,
and they shall be created
and you shall renew the face of the earth.

MEDITATION
Read Ezekiel 37

The sacred way ADVENT 2/MONDAY

◆◆◆

Strengthen all weary hands,
steady all trembling knees
and say to all faint hearts,
'Courage! Do not be afraid.
Look, your God is coming,
vengeance is coming,
the retribution of God;
he is coming to save you.'
Then the eyes of the blind will be opened,
the ears of the deaf unsealed,
then the lame shall leap like a deer
and the tongues of the dumb sing for joy;
For water gushes in the desert,
streams in the wasteland,
the scorched earth becomes a lake,
the parched land springs of water...
And through it will run a highway undefiled
which shall be called the Sacred Way;
the unclean may not travel by it,
nor fools stray along it.

(Isaiah 35:3–8)

Here again scripture communicates to us through the simple things of nature, giving us pictures and images to reflect on. One of the deepest impressions made on me, when I visited the Holy Land, was to see these biblical images at their source, as it were: in the middle of the parched, sun-scorched desert you can certainly grasp the impact gushing streams of water make. (Modern Israel has achieved this in certain areas and you can see the desert blooming with life and fruitfulness.)

Another essentially scriptural image that's based on the desert is 'the way'—in that treacherous landscape, the road beaten out by generations of caravans and leading to a town or oasis meant the difference between life and death for the traveller. It is therefore a vivid symbol of the spiritual life. God himself maps out the way and constantly calls on his people to tread it: he leads and guides those who follow, provides for the journey, is even willing tenderly to carry us along it if we let him. The Lord your God 'carried you, as a man carries his child, all along the road you travelled' (Deuteronomy 1:31). The infant Christian Church under persecution actually described its secret members as 'followers of the Way'.

We can trace this imagery back to Abraham, who took all his family, flocks and possessions, left the security of his homeland and embarked on a nomadic existence of total trust. The theme of 'the way' finds its fullest expression, I think, in Exodus. The people's belief was constantly tested, but it was there in that vast and terrible wilderness that they learnt (often by their mistakes) to understand God's greatness and power to save them from their enemies.

You and I are invited to make the same journey, out of the darkness of an unbelieving world into the promised land of eternal peace and full union with God. On the exodus Moses merely foreshadowed the one true mediator between God and man—Jesus. He is our leader and intimate companion on the way; he provides all we need for the journey, leads us to still waters to revive us, and when we labour too much or carry too many burdens, says 'Come to me, I will give you rest'. He is the light that illuminates the path, and should we stray off it, he will leave the others and search till he finds us.

Why is it that, in spite of this, we are often such reluctant travellers, with weary hands, trembling knees and faint hearts? Let's look at what is involved, and try to find some of the answers to our faint-heartedness. The sacred way calls for radical commitment to the sacraments, prayer, scripture, repentance; but the further away we are from God the harder it is to feel our need of these things. If we go back to the exodus we find that Pharaoh is the symbol of Satan, who will do all he can to prevent us following the way. Like the people whose spirit was crushed, 'so cruel was their bondage', and would not listen to Moses' pleas, so the further we are distanced from God the more spiritually deaf we become; anyone in bondage to something really destructive like drug addiction or alcohol is incapable of hearing any kind of reason, but the same principle applies also to lesser preoccupations.

What Pharaoh does, when he fears that the people will finally listen to Moses' pleas, is to double their workload. That's very significant. If for instance you are trying to deepen your relationship with God in prayer by finding time each day for quiet and reflection—I guarantee you won't find that time, to start with! There'll always be a million things to do (and I speak from experience). It isn't a struggle to watch my favourite TV programme: whatever else I want to do can wait. But if I want to *pray*, there are inevitably urgent and pressing things that must be attended to.

It's all very subtle. But if we can become spiritually aware of what we're dealing with, we can simply pray for the strength to make prayer a priority. A preoccupation with business means 'weary hands', and I find Jesus' powerful admonition helpful—when he refers to hands (as symbolic of work) he says, 'If your right hand offends you, cut it off!' Our decision for God must be as radical as that: we must be positive in our determination to turn from—to die to—superfluous activity, to learn to lean on him all along the road. 'Look, your God is coming. He is coming to save you.'

Remember, the Hebrew slaves didn't understand what God could do for them at first, but they learned *on the way*. If we are willing to get up and follow the sacred way, our eyes will be opened, our ears unstopped, our weak knees will learn to leap like deer, and joy and praise will be on our lips.

PRAYER
If the Lord does not build the house,
in vain for its builders labour;
if the Lord does not watch over the city,
in vain does the watchman keep vigil.
In vain is your earlier rising,
your going later to rest,
you who toil for the bread you eat:
when he pours gifts on his beloved while they slumber.

(Psalm 127[126]:1–2)

MEDITATION
Read Exodus 5:1–14

Consolation on the way

◆◆

'Console my people, console them'
says your God.
'Speak to the heart of Jerusalem
and call to her
that her time of service is ended,
that her sin is atoned for,
that she has received from the hand of the Lord
double punishment for all her crimes'...
... Here is the Lord coming with power,
his arm subduing all things to him.
The prize of his victory is with him,
his trophies all go before him.
He is like a shepherd feeding his flock,
gathering lambs in his arms,
holding them against his breast.

(Isaiah 40:1–2, 10–11)

If we *have* made a decision to walk with God, our constant prayer must be that of the psalmist who pleaded: 'Search me, God, and know my heart. Test me and know my thoughts. See that I follow not the wrong path and lead me in the path of life eternal' (139[138]:23–24). One of the greatest setbacks *en route* are wrong paths, diversions and roadblocks. If we're not (as we discussed last week) keeping watch, we can unknowingly be distracted so that at best we take the longer and more tedious route, at worst lose the way altogether. How can this happen?

The simple, three-letter answer is: sin. Now I happen to believe that the most comforting way to look at the problem of sin is in the light of God's love for us as individuals *where we are*. What makes Mary Magdalene, for me, one of the great saints is the fact that she understood this: she who had seven huge problems with sin (seven demons) was able to fall at the feet of Jesus and accept his healing love for her as she was, where she was. It is pride that says, 'I'll make myself good enough first'. Humility just collapses at his feet, to receive his mercy and healing.

The reading above (taken alongside Matthew 18:12–14) gives us an illuminating picture of God's love and forgiveness. The shepherd is the very personification of love, of attentiveness and protection. His love has no limits, and nothing gives him greater joy than to bring home a sheep that is lost. In Ezekiel 34 we are told how he deals with his lost sheep: 'I shall look for the lost one, bring back the stray, bandage the wounded and make the weak strong' (v. 16).

Isaiah's message is that a time of exile or testing will be followed by a time of comfort and consolation: our sins are atoned for and he holds us close to his heart. I'm sure that it's only in this context of God's mercy that we can begin to come to terms with our own sinfulness—and modern psychology would bear this out. Healing is more likely to take place if someone suffering from emotional problems is given reassurance, rather than admonition and accusation. The trouble is that we are all sinners, we all need inner healing and we live in a maze of interaction. My deep hurt aggravates yours, and yours someone else's. None of us is aware of the root cause of the other's problem—and rarely of our own—so that we are prisoners in a chain of negative reactions.

But belief is what can shatter the prison bars. Jesus points to a 'way out', through a commitment to follow the way (discipleship), then through a commitment to a relationship with God in prayer. As we pray, we begin to understand the infinite love of the shepherd (his 'reassurance'), and in the light of that love we are gradually able to face ourselves: to see not only how we sin, but why, and in some cases we will learn that the root causes are not always our fault. He will teach us how to forgive ourselves (very important). Soon the true disciple will find the 'plank in his eye' beginning to be removed, then he in turn will be able to remove the speck from his brother's eye and, who knows, perhaps from countless eyes.

This is the greatest service we can do in the work of establishing the kingdom of God on earth, to be willing to face ourselves with the help of God, who through Jesus is such an infinitely patient shepherd of our souls. We can only help others to be set free if we ourselves are set free—which is what St Paul prayed so eloquently for in Ephesians: that God's power working in us through the Holy Spirit will enable our hidden self to grow strong (3:14–21). When we *know* the love of Christ, we can be filled with the utter fullness of God, and his power working in us will do more than we can ever imagine.

PRAYER

O search me, God, and know my heart.
O test me and know my thoughts.
See that I follow not the wrong path
and lead me in the path of life eternal.

(Psalm 139[138]:23–24)

MEDITATION

Read Matthew 18:12–14

Resting on the way ADVENT 2/WEDNESDAY

◆◆◆

The Lord is an everlasting God,
he created the boundaries of the earth.
He does not grow tired or weary,
his understanding is beyond fathoming.
He gives strength to the wearied,
he strengthens the powerless.
Young men may grow tired and weary,
youths may stumble,
but those who hope in the Lord
renew their strength,
they put out wings like eagles.

(Isaiah 40:28–31)

'Come to me, all you who labour and are overburdened, and I
will give you rest. Shoulder my yoke and learn from me, for I am
gentle and humble in heart, and you will find rest for your souls.'

(Matthew 11:28–29)

Everyone gets weary, and those who are preparing the way of the Lord frequently encounter difficulties, discouragements, and circumstances beyond their control which prevent them making any real progress. To borrow the analogy of the psalmist, we can so easily get caught in 'the snare of the fowler that seeks to destroy', immobilising those eagle's wings that can carry us away from all harm.

Our progress towards spiritual maturity involves recognising how to face up to and deal with our enemies—and first of course identifying them. It isn't human enemies we are struggling against but (as St Paul tells us in Ephesians 6) 'the spiritual army of evil'. We need to understand the nature of the spiritual warfare being waged among us, and learn with the strength of God how to 'resist the devil's tactics' (Ephesians 6:11).

The other day we noted Pharaoh's response to Moses' message. The people, when they first heard of the promise of deliverance, rejoiced and 'bowed down and worshipped' God (Exodus 4:31). Pharaoh's reaction to their enthusiasm was, 'Make these men work harder, so they do not have time to listen!' The enemy's tactic is no less effective today: we will only ever begin to hear the word of God when we have learned to *find the time* to make God the number one priority in our lives, and learned to be still before him in prayer. It is only on the eagle's wings of prayer that we will be able to soar above the noise and pressure and speed of human activity.

It might be our job that distracts us, taking on too much, refusing to delegate. Ambition is a total preoccupation. Or we can just as easily be slaves to other concerns, beautiful homes, immaculate gardens, endless rounds of entertaining. Or if we are committed Christians our 'work'—even more subtly—might be justified with a label marked 'worthy'. An endless cycle of parish work, Bible-study groups, fund-raising committees can be just as impregnable a barrier to prayer. A nice bit of four-figure fund-raising can keep people busy for years, enslaving them to 'achievement'. Then, again, one of the most seductive monopolies on our time (and I speak from personal experience) is that of 'helping others', to gain acceptance and esteem. If one is not careful, the self-appointed healer and comforter can find themselves far from raising up 'those crawling on their bellies in the dust' but simply keeping them company. If they complain '... but I can't hear God in my prayers', it's probably because they are utterly exhausted from everyone else's problems.

Today's reading, then, is an opportune reminder of the beneficial effects of stopping and listening to God in prayer. If we work backwards we'll often find that the reason for an over-burdened life can be pride, and the cause of that pride simply a lack of self-acceptance, a fear of not being good enough. Therefore an enormous amount of energy is expended on the effort to be somebody loved, accepted and highly thought-of. But Jesus says, 'Come to me with all the burden of activity and pressure. Let me teach you how special and unique you are, created because a loving father wanted to create *you*.' This is how to find rest and security—in the knowledge that we are totally loved by God as we are. We can not earn something we already have. In the light of that love, we can begin to accept ourselves, understand human weakness, and thereby discover the safest way to escape the fowler's snare. That way is the way of humility, which understands that the only true source of strength is God himself.

PRAYER

My soul, give thanks to the Lord
and never forget all his blessings.
It is he who forgives all your guilt,
who heals every one of your ills,
who redeems your life from the grave,
who crowns you with love and compassion,
who fills your life with good things
renewing your youth like an eagle's.

(Psalm 103[102]:2–5)

MEDITATION

Read Psalm 139[138]

From Eve to Mary   ADVENT 2/THURSDAY

◆◆◆

[After Adam had eaten of the tree, the Lord God called to him.]
'Where are you?' he asked. 'I heard the sound of you in the
garden,' he replied. 'I was afraid because I was naked, so I hid.'
'Who told you that you were naked?' he asked. 'Have you been
eating of the tree I forbade you to eat?' The man replied, 'It was
the woman you put with me; she gave me the fruit, and I ate it.'
Then the Lord God asked the woman, 'What is this you have
done?' The woman replied, 'The serpent tempted me and I ate'.
Then the Lord God said to the serpent:
'Because you have done this,
Be accursed beyond all cattle,
all wild beasts.
You shall crawl on your belly and eat dust
every day of your life.
I will make you enemies of each other:
you and the woman,
your offspring and her offspring.
It will crush your head
and you will strike its heel.'

(Genesis 3:9–15)

Today we look first at the famous story of man's downfall, then at the solution.
Our reflection centres on two women, Eve and Mary, both representing a
choice: to choose or not to choose God. It is an option that faces each and every
one of us—in choosing God we choose eternal life, not choosing God we
deliberately choose death (Deuteronomy 30:15–20). We were created in the
image of our creator to be one with him, to share his eternity, to fill and conquer
the earth (Genesis 1). All this with one proviso, that we allow him to be who he
is—the sovereign Lord of creation—and to accept that we are creatures whom
he has chosen to create in his own loving purpose. We are born with a human
nature, not divine but with potential to become divine and a free will that can
choose to respond or not to God.

It might be instructive if we think of mankind, in the beginning, as a new-born baby struggling for life and strength, eyes as yet unfocused, only by instinct discerning the lifeline that will feed and nurture it. It has to learn to suckle and gain its strength from this lifeline, it has to battle for growth. This is humanity's struggle for God. I think this beginning is captured most beautifully by Michelangelo in the Sistine Chapel where he depicts creation in the form of two hands stretching out to each other, one God's, the other Adam's ('man'): the fingers are *almost* touching. It is a most moving vision because, for me, the final picture in our future will be when those two hands are clasped tightly, fingers interlocked, Man and God eternally one.

To pick up our analogy, today's reading shows us that the baby made a bad start, refusing its lifeline, and exercising its God-given freedom. It chose independence of God, the taproot of all sin. (We need not concern ourselves with the question of whether or not Adam and Eve 'existed'; the relevance of the teaching lies in not who they were but what they represent.) If we look at the whole text we find Eve's problem is actually a crisis of belief. She has heard the word of God—saying in essence, 'Don't do that because it's harmful'—but she also hears the tempter undermining the word of God. 'Did God *really* say that...?' We still hear it today: 'Did God *really* mean keep the Sabbath holy... no adultery...?' And mankind, like a child not understanding the discipline of a loving father, still can't believe that God really *did* mean it. Then he has let go of the lifeline and is on a course for disaster that's of his own choosing.

'The serpent tempted me and I ate.' It is a horrifying thought, except for the note of optimism in the story: one day the head of the serpent will be crushed by the offspring of the woman, man will overcome his enemy. Our destiny hasn't changed; we have suffered a setback but eventually God and man will co-operate in defeating the enemy. Through all the conflict and drama of the growth of belief in the Old Testament, we do find the hand of man continually reaching upwards, and God's hand still reaching down. A remnant of the people of Israel kept alive a hope of redemption, and this incredible hope began to be realised on the day a virgin daughter of this people said yes to God. Like Eve she was human, like you and me she was ordinary, but she quietly and simply *believed* in the word of God and agreed to co-operate with his plan for mankind's redemption. She may not have understood the angel's message, but she understood who God is. This is the central Advent message—nothing is impossible to God, in *my* life as well as Mary's. This is why the Church refers to Mary as the new Eve. Eve doubted the word of God and the result was death; Mary believed and the result was life for all mankind.

During the last week of Advent we will be hearing more of Mary, but today we need to commit ourselves to seeking a deeper understanding of who God is, and pray for a heightened awareness of his greatness which can transform ordinary human lives. When we begin to experience the word of God made flesh in us too, so will we be able to rejoice with Mary: 'My soul proclaims the greatness of the Lord and my spirit exults in God my saviour'.

PRAYER

Sing a new song to the Lord
for he has worked wonders.
His right hand and his holy arm
have brought salvation.

(Psalm 98[97]:1)

MEDITATION
Read all of chapter 3 of Genesis, side by side
with Luke 1:26–38

The way of the world

◆◆

Happy indeed is the man
who follows not the counsel of the wicked;
nor lingers in the way of sinners
nor sits in the company of scorners,
but whose delight is the law of the Lord
and who ponders his law day and night.
He is like a tree that is planted
beside the flowing waters,
that yields its fruit in due season
and whose leaves shall never fade;
and all that he does shall prosper.

(Psalm 1:1–3)

For me the greatest prayer-book ever written is the Book of Psalms—the prayer-book of Israel. Although these Hebrew poems and songs date right back to the time of David, they have been constantly prayed, sung and recited through the centuries and, still today, are central to the prayers of the Christian Church. In them we find every form of human expression, every emotion; man's entire experience of life and his relationship with God is catalogued among these prayers.

Some people find their first approach to prayer through the psalms difficult. While Christian emphasis is on loving our neighbour, the psalmist seems to be forever plotting his neighbour's downfall! Lines like 'O God, that you would slay the wicked!... I hate them with a perfect hate...' (139[138]:19, 22). But we must remember that they were written in the context of a primitive people struggling with an embryonic relationship of faith in the one true God. This struggle was constantly under threat from invading armies, pagan peoples who worshipped idols, and the one true faith had to be defended according to the primitive understanding of human rights, which were established or surrendered on the battlefield. The whole of the Old Testament is the testimony of a nation, born like a tiny baby, grappling for growth and life, and slowly maturing to a point in history when it has to graduate into a new era, when the God it has sought comes to them in person with a message of peace.

When he entered Jerusalem Jesus wept because the people had not understood this message. His prophecy about its destruction was fulfilled: for 2,000 years the Jewish people have had no homeland, and even since their historic return in our own time we are still witness to Christ's words, 'Your enemies will encircle you and hem you in on every side' (Luke 19:43). Even now nations, Christian and Jewish, misunderstand Christ's message of peace and put their trust in weapons and warfare.

If we return to the psalms with the benefit of this hindsight, we can see the wisdom of the Holy Spirit transcending the human battlefield and taking us into the realms of spiritual battles, where the enemies are more real and significant. These are 'the Sovereignties and the Powers who originate the darkness in this world' (Ephesians 6:12) and today we can be as heartfelt as the psalmist in pleading for deliverance. After the resurrection Jesus explained (Luke 24:44) that the writings in the psalms were about himself, and indeed his cry on the cross was the cry of Psalm 22[21]: 'My God, my God, why have you forsaken me?' For Christians the prophetic voice of the psalmist finds a new dimension.

Reading Psalm 1 as a whole (and including vv. 4–6) we find it continues the familiar biblical theme of choosing 'the way'. There are always two choices: a choice, as Deuteronomy 30 puts it quite plainly, between life or death. The psalmist characterises it as the way of the Lord (which is life-giving and prosperous) or the way of the wicked (which is judgement and doom). For those who follow the Lord's way the author puts emphasis on two things: detachment and prayer. First he draws our attention to the way of the world, the attitudes of the unbelieving, secular world. We are not to 'linger', meaning: try to compromise our belief to placate the demands of the secular society. We have to be resolute and single-minded when the scorners decry Christian values as out-of-date. If we subscribe to the gospel teaching we *cannot* compromise; we must be detached from the views of the unbelievers whatever the cost.

I once heard a prominent church leader actually say publicly that the gospel teaching on peace was difficult to apply to the political complexities that exist 2,000 years on! This is precisely what the psalmist is warning us against—keeping company with the unbelieving world of power and politics, and adopting its standards. Psalm 1 has the answer: the way to deal with the complexities of our modern life is prayer. The man who ponders on the mystery of God, who finds his delight in the Lord, is opening his life to grace. Like that tree planted beside flowing waters, he draws his strength directly from God and in due season grace (the fruits of growth) goes out to others. In spite of the storms and winds of the world it remains intact, because 'the Lord guards the ways of the just'.

PRAYER

Those who fear the Lord do not disdain his words,
and those who love him keep his ways.
Those who fear the Lord do their best to please him,
and those who love him find satisfaction in his Law.
Those who fear the Lord keep their hearts prepared
and humble themselves in his presence.
Let us fall into the hand of the Lord,
not the hands of men;
for as his majesty is, so too is his mercy.

(Ecclesiasticus 2:15–18)

MEDITATION

Read Psalm 1 side by side with
Deuteronomy 30:15–20

The way down
from the mountain   ADVENT 2/SATURDAY

◆◆◆

As they came down from the mountain... the disciples put this
question to Jesus: 'Why do the scribes say then that Elijah has to
come first?' 'True' he replied; 'Elijah is to come to see that
everything is once more as it should be; however, I tell you that
Elijah has come already and they did not recognise him but
treated him as they pleased; and the Son of Man will suffer
similarly at their hands.' The disciples understood then that he
had been speaking of John the Baptist.

(Matthew 17:9–13)

Peter, James and John were the three disciples Jesus took 'up a high mountain' to witness his suffering, and experience a foretaste of his glorious resurrection. What a moment it must have been for these three who had left everything, to follow in faith and hope a travelling evangelist! They had listened to his preaching, seen his miracles, felt in their hearts that he must be the Messiah: but now he stood transfigured before them. What they had believed in faith now became a glorious reality. Here before them stood the humble carpenter's son of Nazareth transfigured into Lord and Saviour of mankind, and beside him Moses and Elijah (representing the Law and the prophets) affirming that this is indeed the Messiah who is the fulfilment of both.

From the reaction of Peter to this experience (true to form, a very human one) we can learn a great deal. He wanted to build three tents in commemoration (the tent being, throughout the Bible, a symbol of permanence in the desert).

How we can identify with him, we who so often want to hang on to and make permanent our mountain-top experiences of God. If only those sweet encounters could be more permanent! But the next thing Jesus does with these three chosen disciples is take them down from the mountain-top to accompany him on his journey to Calvary. What they have just witnessed *is* the culmination: what lies beyond the sorrow and suffering ahead is the glory of the resurrection.

Then they remember that Elijah is supposed to come first. He has, Jesus explains, in John the Baptist—but, like the great prophet before him, John had to suffer at the hands of men. What this text is spelling out for us is that the path of *true* discipleship cannot be a continual mountain-top experience. It will not be without its moments of consolation and joy—of course there will be plateaus of rest and refreshment—but there will also be sorrow and suffering as an inevitable part of our purification. Not, as some people fear, in the shape of great tragedy and disaster but rather in the willingness constantly to face ourselves.

Like Jesus who set his face towards Jerusalem, we have to be resolute in facing up to ourselves, allowing the Holy Spirit to reveal the root causes of our sinfulness and illuminate the dark areas. Peter, who was full of joy on the mountain (and was to go on to do great things for God), had to go through the pain of real self-knowledge before he could become a true disciple. So it is for us. We can deceive ourselves into thinking we are doing great things for God— but all the time we must watchfully question our motives. For Christians who confine themselves to the circuits of conferences and prayer-meetings, the measure of success tends to be 'What did I get out of it?' While, undoubtedly, our faith is enhanced by witnessing miracles, healing, prophecy and the rest, we must continually ask ourselves the question 'Am I seeking God for himself, or am I seeking him for what he can do for me?'

The way of the cross is the narrow way of turning aside from self. John the Baptist said it: 'He must grow greater, I must grow smaller' (John 3:30). We must be like Jesus, emptied of self. If we are prepared to die to self, we will rise to life and give life to others ('unless a wheat grain falls on the ground and dies, it remains only a single grain; but if it dies, it yields a rich harvest' John 12:24). Let's end today by asking ourselves the question, are we really living in the Spirit, are we allowing him to baptise us with fire, purifying the selfish intentions of our hearts, to re-create us into co-workers for the kingdom? The closer we come to the cross, the closer we approach the resurrection. *Then* we will live permanently in the vision of the mountain-top. 'Blessed are the pure in heart, for they shall see God' (Matthew 5:8).

PRAYER

Deliver us, O Lord, from our bondage
as streams in dry land.
Those who are sowing in tears
will sing when they reap.
They go out, they go out, full of tears,
carrying seed for the sowing:
they come back, they come back, full of song,
carrying their sheaves.

(Psalm 126[125]:4–6)

MEDITATION
Read Matthew 16:24–17:8

In Joyful Hope

In joyful hope

◆◆◆

> *Be patient, brothers, until the Lord's coming. Think of a farmer: how patiently he waits for the precious fruit of the ground until it has had the autumn rains and the spring rains! You too have to be patient; do not lose heart, because the Lord's coming will be soon. Do not make complaints against one another, brothers, so as not to be brought to judgement yourselves; the Judge is already to be seen waiting at the gates. For your example, brothers, in submitting with patience, take the prophets who spoke in the name of the Lord.*
>
> *(James 5:7–10)*

Today the theme of Advent changes: the time of re-awakening and preparation now gives way to a new atmosphere of joy and expectancy. 'The Lord's coming will be soon!' We can begin to anticipate the joy of this coming. 'I have come that you might have life in all its fullness.'

Yes, indeed, but the wisdom of today's reading is that while it points us towards the reality of Christ's coming, at the same time it urges on us another kind of reality, one that is very relevant to the world we find ourselves living in: patience. Anyone observing small children at this time of the year recognises the wonder and bubbling excitement welling up, centred on a story in scripture of a tiny baby born in a manger. Older children may have gifts in mind, but the little ones are fascinated with the Christmas story, singing it, dressing up for it, enacting it, counting the days. The joy of their anticipation is patently real.

But what of us? How do we approach the celebration when we switch on the 9 o'clock news and observe the state of the world two thousand years on? What we see so often is darkness and confusion. I well remember the singers Simon and Garfunkel at the Albert Hall encapsulating the problem in a song: as they sang Silent Night (more beautifully than I'd ever heard it sung) they actually had a BBC newsreader giving out a news bulletin in the background: the contrast was stunning. How, then, do we reconcile this paradox of experiencing the peaceful calm of that silent holy night with the violence and turmoil that surrounds us?

The answer must lie, simply, in our belief—not the fairweather, head-in-the-sand variety, but a belief that squarely faces the reality of what happens in a world that has forgotten God. We must not run from the problem, but respond to it. James exhorts us to learn from the prophets, the faithful remnant, who could not make the people listen to the word of God but proclaimed it nevertheless. They said the Messiah would come to save the world, and he did! And he himself told us that his kingdom would be like a seed planted in the ground, growing imperceptibly in the dark, unseen but *growing*. It would begin as small as a mustard seed, but in the end it would grow bigger than any other tree so that all the birds of the air could shelter in its branches.

So be patient and trust, says James, and wait for the precious fruits. Spring, in the Bible, is often a symbol of salvation; but before we can enjoy the blossom we must wait for autumn and winter to pass. Then we will hear the voice of the Lord, as in the Song of Solomon: 'Come... for see, the winter is past, the rains are over and gone. The flowers appear on the earth. The season of glad joys has come, the cooing of the turtledove is heard in our land. The fig tree is forming its first figs and the blossoming vines give out their fragrance' (2:11–13).

Let us also remember that Jesus comes to us, in the words of the carol, in the midst of the bleak midwinter—in humility and poverty, in suffering and rejection but also ultimately in triumph and victory. To his disciples he said 'You *will* have trouble in the world, but do not be afraid, I have overcome the world' (John 16:33). So as we contemplate the winter landscape of a troubled world, let us not forget that the battle *is* won, the kingdom is established and is within each of us. Therefore we must be prepared to let it grow in us: we must grow in faith and accept the full challenges of a deeper and deeper conversion, as we patiently await with joyful hope the coming of our Saviour.

PRAYER

To you have I lifted up my eyes,
you who dwell in the heavens:
my eyes, like the eyes of slaves
on the hand of their lords.
Like the eyes of a servant
on the hand of her mistress,
so our eyes are on the Lord our God
till he show us his mercy.

(Psalm 123[122]:1–2)

MEDITATION

Read John 16:20–33

Knowing God

◆◆◆

Jesus had gone into the Temple and was teaching, when the chief priests and the elders of the people came to him and said, 'What authority have you for acting like this? And who gave you this authority?' 'And I' replied Jesus, 'will ask you a question, only one; if you tell me the answer to it, I will then tell you my authority for acting like this. John's baptism: where did it come from: heaven or man?' And they argued it out this way among themselves, 'If we say from heaven, he will retort, "Then why did you refuse to believe him?"; but if we say from man, we have the people to fear, for they all hold that John was a prophet'. So their reply to Jesus was, 'We do not know'. And he retorted, 'Nor will I tell you my authority for acting like this'.

(Matthew 21:23–27)

Here we find Matthew's account of the events following Christ's triumphal entry into the city of Jerusalem the previous day (21:1–11), a vivid report of the confrontation between the leaders of the Jewish faith and the Messiah who stood in their midst, unrecognised but so challenging and disturbing that in a few days' time they would put him to death to silence him. The first scene in the Temple which Matthew describes for us is the extraordinary way in which Jesus deals with the commercialism that had infiltrated the Temple: quoting Isaiah he insists that God's house must be a house of *prayer*. Here I'm reminded of a charming—and very enlightening—story which illustrates not so much how providential God is, but how he blesses those who are living in obedience to his word.

I recently visited a country parish where the Anglican vicar and his wife serve two churches. They and their two parish councils some time ago made a courageous decision to do away with all fund-raising. They had the usual problems of repair and upkeep, nevertheless they decided to step out in faith. No more bazaars, fetes, bring-and-buys, coffee mornings or sponsored anythings. Instead they would have family prayer-meetings, and would try to bring the community together at a few supper evenings and invite a speaker to give the people some spiritual help. What I saw at one of these were people working together, as at a bazaar but with the essential difference that here their one object was 'to know the Lord better'. The net result, I'm happy to tell you, is that the parish's income has increased 50 per cent in the first year, and what they haven't needed has been donated to a local hospice. And that's not all: in the last year several new young people have joined the congregation. I found it a wonderful witness to the truth of Jesus' words, 'seek ye first the kingdom of God, and all then will be added'.

However, back to the Temple. Notice that in this whole exchange with the chief priests Jesus never attempts to justify either his words or his actions: he simply *has* the authority of his Father in heaven. Indeed with a very few words it is their authority—not his—that is challenged in front of all the people. The key phrase in this scene is 'they did not know'. They didn't know who John the Baptist was, they didn't know they had God incarnate standing before them: they were spiritually deaf and spiritually blind (Jesus actually addresses them as 'blind guides'). In spite of the tradition of the scriptures and the prophets handed down since Abraham, they would not allow the word of God to penetrate their hearts.

It's clear from this passage, and from other parts of the Gospel narratives where Jesus compares the religious hypocrite to the open-minded repentant sinner, that what comes most severely under God's judgement is hypocrisy—religious play-acting—and especially among leaders who are responsible for shaping the spiritual lives of others ('Teachers' warns James in his letter, 'can expect a stricter judgement!' 3:1). But the solution to religious hypocrisy is seeking to *know God*, in the Church, in the eucharist, in scripture, learning to listen in the quietness of prayer to the still small voice: 'be still and *know* that I am God' (Psalm 46[45]:10).

Only in prayer will *we* recognise Jesus in the day-to-day circumstances of our lives and the lives of others. And this positive knowledge can transform us—someone who knows the reality of the living God is someone who speaks and acts with his authority. 'All authority in heaven and on earth has been given to me. Go, therefore, make disciples of all the nations: baptise them in the name of the Father and of the Son and of the Holy Spirit, and teach them to observe all the commands I gave you. And *know* that I am with you always; yes, to the end of time' (Matthew 28:18–20).

PRAYER

Lord, make me know your ways.
Lord, teach me your paths.
Make me walk in your truth, and teach me:
for you are God my saviour.

(Psalm 25[24]:4–5)

MEDITATION
Read Matthew 23

The humble way

◆◆

I, the Lord your God,
I am holding you by the right hand;
I tell you, 'Do not be afraid,
I will help you'.
Do not be afraid, Jacob poor worm,
Israel puny mite.
I will help you—it is the Lord who speaks—
the Holy One of Israel is your redeemer.

(Isaiah 41:13–14)

'What is your opinion? A man had two sons. He went and said
to the first, "My boy, you go and work in the vineyard today". He
answered, "I will not go", but afterwards thought better of it and
went. The man then went and said the same thing to the second
who answered, "Certainly, sir", but did not go. Which of the two
did the father's will?' 'The first' they said. Jesus said to them, 'I
tell you solemnly, tax collectors and prostitutes are making their
way into the kingdom of God before you'.

(Matthew 21:28–31)

Today's readings invite us to contrast two human conditions: pride and humility. All through the Bible we find that God always favours the humble: 'My eyes are drawn to the man of humble and contrite spirit' (Isaiah 66:2). But when he has to deal with pride, we can observe the full force of his anger—not least in the dialogue (above) between Jesus and the Pharisees. What Jesus is telling the Jewish religious leaders here is that those who arrogantly say 'yes' to God simply as an outward show impress him not at all. But the ones who perhaps doubt their ability at first, who understand their own frailty, these are the ones who make progress in the spiritual life and quietly make their way into the kingdom.

Contrast this uncompromising attitude with that described by Isaiah above, and we find a very different tone altogether. Here is a picture of a loving, caring father, totally reassuring a helpless child. This acknowledgement of the child's helplessness ('poor, puny mite'), far from being accusing or contemptuous, is full of endearment. I have come across a similar expression in Italy—where all adult hearts seem to melt instantly in the presence of tiny children: the word they use is 'poverino' or 'poor little one', but always said with great affection and love.

If we try to see ourselves through God's eyes, this is how we *ought* to look: precious but puny mites. If we could only grasp this and learn to relate to God in our poverty and helplessness, allowing him to help us, we would become saints overnight! If we want to make lighter work of the spiritual journey, there is a 'shortcut' called the humble way. But how do we find it?

First of all we can only begin to see our own poverty if we're willing to come closer to God himself: our weakness is only revealed in the light of his absolute holiness. We say we believe in God almighty... but do we understand just what almighty means? When Isaiah had a vision of God whose glory filled all heaven and earth, his reaction says everything: 'What a wretched state I am in!' When John the Baptist saw Jesus standing before him he could only concede that now 'He must grow greater and I must grow smaller'. We too, if we are serious in seeking God, must begin to understand his greatness and our own smallness.

How easy this would be if only we were willing to accept the truth. But pride distorts the truth, deceives us into thinking we have to follow the spiritual way entirely through our own effort, doing something for God, being something for God, slaving away to earn salvation. Jesus himself illustrated the problem with the parable of the Pharisee and the tax collector (Luke 18:9–14)—the Pharisee thanks God he is not like other men and proceeds to reel off his list of impressive achievements; the tax collector on the other hand 'hardly dares raise his eyes' in reverence. In three very important respects he should be a pattern for us: in his awareness of *(i)* the greatness of God, *(ii)* our own poverty, and *(iii)* God's forgiving love. He also had a large dose of something we all desperately need, and that's courage—courage to come before a loving God and face up to his need for him. The tax collector found peace and security in that love, because he went home at rights with God. 'He who humbles himself will be exalted' said Jesus.

For me the very personification of this teaching was the young French nun, St Thérèse of Lisieux, whose autobiography continues to be my own most treasured spiritual book. She understood what Jesus meant when he said we must become like little children. Her form of spirituality she called 'the little way': bypassing the lofty spiritual teaching she didn't understand, she became small and hidden, living a life of childlike trust in God. Though she died at the age of 24, she became one of the greatest witnesses to the gospel in modern times. Her exposition may be too simple for some, but I find it completely in keeping with the Bible's teaching—and with the picture painted so vividly by Isaiah above. 'When I turn to the sacred scriptures' wrote St Thérèse, 'then all becomes clear—a single word opens out new vistas, perfection appears easy, and I see it is enough to acknowledge one's nothingness and surrender oneself like a child into God's arms' (*Story of a Soul*).

PRAYER

In the Lord my soul shall take its boast.
The humble shall hear and be glad...
[The just] call and the Lord hears
and rescues them in all their distress.
The Lord is close to the broken-hearted;
those whose spirit is crushed he will save.

(Psalm 34[33]:2, 17–18)

MEDITATION

Read Isaiah 41:8–14 (pray each line slowly,
inserting your own name in place of Israel or
Jacob)

As we wait

◆◆

John, summoning two of his disciples, sent them to the Lord to ask, 'Are you the one who is to come, or must we wait for someone else?' When the men reached Jesus they said, 'John the Baptist has sent us to you, to ask, "Are you the one who is to come or have we to wait for someone else?"' It was just then that he cured many people of diseases and afflictions and of evil spirits, and gave the gift of sight to many who were blind. Then he gave the messengers their answer, 'Go back and tell John what you have seen and heard: the blind see again, the lame walk, lepers are cleansed, and the deaf hear, the dead are raised to life, the Good News is proclaimed to the poor and happy is the man who does not lose faith in me'.

(Luke 7:18–23)

Today's reading from the Gospels gives us a glimpse, I think, of the prevailing air of joyful expectancy among those who had been listening to John the Baptist and to Jesus. We know from an earlier account in St Luke that all sorts of people had come to John—including tax collectors and soldiers—and there had been growing speculation as to whether John was the Christ. John's reply to that was 'Someone is coming, someone more powerful than I' (Luke 3:16). John, the last and greatest of the messianic prophets, himself echoed what all the prophets had foretold: that the Messiah was to be known by his saving power. Victory over sin and death, sickness and disease would be the sign of his authority.

In the light of Matthew's assertion that John recognised Jesus when he came himself for baptism, there would seem on the face of it to be a contradiction in today's reading. Why send disciples to enquire of someone you had already acknowledged? The answer is probably quite simple: there had to be a transition period when John's own disciples were to leave him and follow Jesus. Apart from the initial confusion between the two, there must have been a deep sense of loyalty among John's followers, some of whom might have been reluctant to desert him—particularly as he was now in Herod's prison. My own feeling is that John, very wisely, sent his disciples to see for themselves who Jesus was, and to be reassured in the knowledge that the kingdom he had been proclaiming was being established before their eyes.

How good the news must have sounded to John in the darkness of his prison cell! The more we get to the heart of scripture the better we can understand that the characters we read about were all human beings just like us. John, who had devoted his life to prayer and fasting to prepare people for the coming of Jesus, is apparently rewarded with incarceration and impending death. But then comes the message of hope: don't worry, everything is going to plan—death is not the end, even the dead are raised to life. *'Happy is the man who does not lose faith in me.'*

As we continue to prepare for the coming of the Messiah, we too should be full of expectant hope. As we get ready to celebrate this new birth, it must happen that the word will become flesh within us, opening our eyes and ears to the wonder of what God means to us. It's ironic, really, that more than at any other time of this year we are likely to have less time for God during this hallowed season—and I speak from bitter experience. For years I have been a slave to the pride of perfection: all the Christmas cards *must* be sent, the parcels beautifully wrapped, and hours spent agonising over whether so-and-so would like this or that. I have in effect spent my Advent in a panic. No matter how hard I worked, so-and-so already had such and such (and I didn't send cards to the people I received them from!).

One of the ways in which we can follow John's message of repentance is to be prepared to fail, to be humble enough to opt out of what the world makes of Christmas, to make a radical pruning of our 'Christmas' activities. We need to give ourselves time to reflect on this great mystery of how it can be that almighty God can take human flesh, and as a man communicate directly to men the message of eternal life. It is a tragedy that in the 1990s man finds himself preoccupied instead with tinsel and wrapping paper, running in a race against time that only ends when the key is turned on the last cash register on Christmas Eve. Twenty-four hours later all our efforts—like the wrapping paper—are torn up and forgotten and we watch the queues for the January sales assembling on our TV screens! What we're really anticipating and awaiting in joyful hope is liberation from that kind of slavery. So let us pray for the wisdom to ponder this great mystery we are about to celebrate, and to be lovingly attentive to its meaning and purpose in our lives.

PRAYER

I will hear what the Lord God has to say,
a voice that speaks of peace,
peace for his people and his friends
and those who turn to him in their hearts.
His help is near for those who fear him
and his glory will dwell in our land.

(Psalm 85[84]:8–9)

MEDITATION

Read Isaiah 52:7–10

The joy of loving

◆◆

Do not be afraid, you will not be put to shame,
do not be dismayed, you will not be disgraced;
for you will forget the shame of your youth...
For now your creator will be your husband...
Yes, like a forsaken wife, distressed in spirit,
the Lord calls you back...
I did forsake you for a brief moment,
but with great love will I take you back.
In excess of anger, for a moment
I hid my face from you.
But with the everlasting love I have taken pity
on you,
says the Lord, your redeemer...
for the mountains may depart,
the hills be shaken,
but my love for you will never leave you.

(Isaiah 54:4–10)

All we can do, when we approach a reading such as this, is pray for ears to hear—in the Hebrew sense that is, hear with our hearts. Not for the first time in the Bible God here compares himself with a husband deeply in love with an erring wife. He cannot put up with her infidelity, yet his love is so strong his anger is eclipsed by it. He longs for her to return: whatever her guilt his love redeems it.

Ruth Burrows, one of my favourite modern spiritual writers, says in her autobiography *Before the Living God* that 'the whole meaning of our existence and the one consuming desire of the heart of God is that we let ourselves be loved'. It's an extraordinary statement when you think about it, yet it is borne out completely by scripture—it is just that it is hard for us to accept this truth in our guilt-ridden state. The enemy the Book of Revelation refers to as 'the accuser of our brethren' points his finger at us and says, not you, you're not good enough—and we feebly try to raise *ourselves* up from the dust and *make* ourselves good enough. Subconsciously we want to redeem ourselves first, and then let God in on the act.

Yet the husband loves the wife *in* her unfaithfulness. She doesn't have to prove herself faithful to earn his love. Even though his anger blazes for a moment, his intense love blots out the faults. 'Do not be afraid, you will not be put to shame. With great love I will take you back.' Love, and love alone, can cancel out sin. All we are called upon to do is allow that love to get to us. What prevents it is pride, like a cosmetic sticking-plaster on an unhealed wound.

Those who cannot respond to the challenge of love tend to harden their hearts to it, like the scribes and Pharisees who hid their fears behind an organised show of human strength. It is worth noting that in Matthew's account of the confrontation between Jesus and the scribes and Pharisees (which we have been considering earlier this week), after his scathing attack on their conduct it ends with a rather plaintive sigh of love: 'Jerusalem... how often have I longed to gather your children, as a hen gathers her chicks under wings, and you refused!' (Matthew 23:37).

'My love will never leave you'. We must cling to this truth whatever our sins, past or present. As we prepare to celebrate the coming of Jesus, we need to remind ourselves that he came for sinners. Unlike the Pharisees who couldn't face their own sinfulness and receive forgiveness, we must try to banish pretence and be honest about our unfaithfulness. Rejecting his love, we may well come under the judgement of his anger like the unfaithful wife—but it will be to reveal our foolishness and bring us back to himself. 'The hills may be shaken, but my love for you will never leave you.'

PRAYER
Sing psalms to the Lord, you who love him,
give thanks to his holy name.
His anger lasts but a moment; his favour through life.
At night there are tears, but joy comes with dawn...
The Lord listened and had pity.
The Lord came to my help.
For me you have changed
my mourning into dancing...
O Lord my God, I will thank you for ever.

(Psalm 30[29]:4–5, 10–12)

MEDITATION
Read Hosea 2:8–20[10–22]

For all the peoples   ADVENT 3/FRIDAY
◆◆◆

*Foreigners who have attached themselves to the Lord to serve him
and to love his name and be his servants—all who observe the
sabbath, not profaning it, and cling to my covenant—these I will
bring to my holy mountain. I will make them joyful in my house
of prayer. Their holocausts and their sacrifices will be accepted on
my altar, for my house will be called a house of prayer for all the
peoples.*

(Isaiah 56:6–7)

One of the things that never fails to impress me about the word of God
spoken through the prophets is that it is quite unequivocal. When God
proclaims his word, there are never any 'ifs' or 'buts' or 'maybes'. 'Your word,
O Lord' says Psalm 118, 'for ever stands firm'. And so it is with today's reading,
which has much to say to us about the ultimate unity of believers. It isn't so
much a question of how it is to happen, or when: it is as it were already signed
and sealed. 'My house will be a house of prayer *for all the peoples.'*

One of the greatest shortcomings of modern Christendom is its fragmented
and divisive nature. Far from putting up a united front against the continual
secularisation of our society and the encroaching tide of atheism, the kingdom
is 'divided against itself' (Matthew 12:25). It sometimes seems to me that the
only spiritual nourishment many of our children get nowadays is from the fringes
of the occult—not least, I have to say, on breakfast TV with its analysis of 'the
stars', fortune-telling of a kind that denies God. One of the most chillingly
prophetic voices in our time, Alexander Solzhenitsyn, has spoken powerfully on
this theme: in a lecture entitled 'Men have forgotten God', he warned that the
threat of godless Communism was so serious that mankind was heading for
catastrophe. 'In recent years' he says, 'the major Christian churches have taken
steps towards reconciliation, but these measures are far too slow: the world is
perishing a hundred times more quickly'. He goes on: while the 'noose on the
neck of mankind grows tighter' Christians must provide 'a united front against
atheism'.

If Christians remain entrenched in their isolated denominations we must be
prepared to face the consequences of this gathering evil of unbelief. If we are not
prepared to heed Christ's prayer 'may they all be one... so that the world may

believe' (John 17), we are collectively *and* individually responsible for the spread of atheism. Unity begins with me. Is my heart open enough to forget the divisions of the past and accept with joy the rich fruits of another tradition, which will enhance and enliven my own? Anyone who professes Jesus Christ is my brother and sister. 'His commandments are these: that we believe in the name of his Son Jesus Christ and that we *love one another as he told us to*' (1 John 3:23).

Our reading for today—Isaiah's vision of all people being united in joyful prayer on the mountain of Israel—actually calls for us to look further in our search for unity than just the Christian Church. Gentiles, he is saying, will be accepted into the house of prayer (i.e. unity with God) as well as, not *instead* of, God's people Israel. Here is the central pivot of unity, the point where the old covenant and the new join forces and fulfil that ancient promise in Genesis 12:3, 'All the tribes of the earth shall bless themselves by you'. As we, in Advent, celebrate the first coming of the Messiah and look towards his final glorious coming, the people of Israel are experiencing the very same Advent—for they also await the coming of the Messiah! Since 1947 part of Ezekiel's prophecy has been fulfilled: 'I am going to take the sons of Israel from the nations where they have gone... and bring them home to their own soil...' The other part remains, '... and one king is to be king of them all' (37:21–22). We *and* they await the one King, for as St Paul reminds us: Christ came 'from their flesh and blood' (Romans 9:5) and we Christians are grafted onto and supported by the root Israel (11:18).

We must constantly pray, as children of Abraham, for reconciliation between Christian and Christian, and between Christian and Jew—without whom there would be no sacred scriptures, no prophets, no House of David, no Mary, no Jesus. We must be humble and learn to reach out, to ask for forgiveness for all that has divided us. 'There can be no ecumenism worthy of the name without a change of heart. For it is from newness of attitudes, from self-denial and unstinted love that yearnings for unity grow towards maturity' (Vatican II).

PRAYER

*O God, be gracious and bless us
and let your face shed its light upon us.
So will your ways be known upon earth
and all nations learn your saving help.*

(Psalm 67[66]:1–2)

MEDITATION

Read Romans 11

The lion and the lamb ADVENT 3/SATURDAY

> *Jacob called his sons and said...*
> *'Gather round, sons of Jacob, and listen;*
> *listen to Israel your father...*
> *Judah, your brothers shall praise you:*
> *you grip your enemies by the neck,*
> *your father's sons shall do you homage.*
> *Judah is a lion cub...*
> *The sceptre shall not pass from Judah,*
> *nor the mace from between his feet,*
> *until he come to whom it belongs,*
> *to whom the peoples shall render obedience.'*

(Genesis 49:1–2,8–10)

Today, and over the next seven days, the season of Advent reaches its climax; a positive air of expectancy is generated through the Church's prayers and readings, which give expression to the deep longing for God to come and save us. Up to now we have been searching the roots of our faith and found from the scriptures that it always leads us to Jesus, the Christ, the one who is to 'come'. The Old Testament ends (Malachi 4:2[3:20]) with a promise that the sun of righteousness will shine out with healing in its rays; the New Testament begins with the birth of Jesus, supported in both Matthew and Luke by a genealogy— a link with what has gone before. Matthew, writing specifically for Jews, takes it back as far as Abraham while Luke, a Gentile, gives his family-tree a more universal flavour by going back to Adam.

Today's reading fits into this pattern. It is taken from the chapter in Genesis where the dying Jacob passes on the traditional blessing to his twelve sons, who will give their names to the twelve tribes of Israel. It can scarcely be termed a prophecy but it is interesting to note that the area later known as Judaea was named after Judah and his tribe, and its inhabitants called Jews. Seven hundred years before Christ the prophet Micah (a contemporary of Isaiah) prophesied about the birthplace of the Messiah: 'But you, Bethlehem, the least of the clans of Judah, out of you will be born for me the one who is to rule over Israel' (5:2).

Jacob's dying wish is to be buried in Canaan with his forefathers Abraham and Isaac—and today at Hebron in Judaea there are three monuments commemorating the burial-places of the three great fathers of Israel—but at the time his semi-nomadic family had fled famine to live in the land of the great Pharaoh, which would seem to make Jacob's assertions of kingly strength slightly incongruous. Yet in the Book of Revelation, John's vision of the one who is to open the scroll (as the one who has triumphed) is of the 'Lion of the tribe of Judah, the Root of David'—a royal king with the strength of a lion. But what John actually sees—and this is the truly revealing symbolism—is neither a lion nor a king but a sacrificial lamb (Revelation 5).

Jesus, the sun of righteousness, on whom the spirit of wisdom, counsel and power dwells (Isaiah 11), in fact describes *himself* in the Gospels with only two words, humble and gentle. In his strength is gentleness, and these are precisely the signs by which in our own time we can recognise those who are responding to God in their lives. As St Paul says, their inner self begins to grow strong but the strength is accompanied by great gentleness and serenity, a deep peace that 'passes all understanding' (Philippians 4:7).

During the last seven days of Advent seven ancient prayers of the Church are recited during evening prayer. They are called the great 'O' Antiphons, each one picking out a symbolic image of the Messiah in the Old Testament and pleading with him to 'Come' (also derived from these prayers is the great Advent hymn, O come, O come Emmanuel). The poignant cry, 'O come', epitomises the deep longing for union between man and God: throughout the Old Testament God pleaded with man to come to him, now his people respond by crying out to him 'O come!'

Each year, as we approach the season of new birth and new life, we must pray that God will come to *us* in a meaningful way. Whether we know him very little or very well, he always has more of himself to give us, more to say to us, more to teach us. From now until Christmas we will end our reflections with one of these great solemn prayers.

PRAYER

O Wisdom, you come forth from the most high.
You fill the universe and hold all things together
in a strong yet gentle manner.
O come, to teach us the way of truth.

MEDITATION
Read Revelation 5

O Come!

Joseph

◆◆

*This is how Jesus Christ came to be born. His mother Mary was
betrothed to Joseph; but before they came to live together she was
found to be with child through the Holy Spirit. Her husband,
Joseph, being a man of honour and wanting to spare her
publicity, decided to divorce her informally. He had made up his
mind to do this when the angel of the Lord appeared to him in a
dream and said, 'Joseph son of David, do not be afraid to take
Mary home as your wife, because she has conceived what is in her
by the Holy Spirit. She will give birth to a son and you must
name him Jesus, because he is the one who is to save his people
from their sins.' Now all this took place to fulfil the words spoken
by the Lord through the prophet: 'The virgin will conceive and
give birth to a son and they will call him Immanuel, a name
which means "God-is-with-us"'. When Joseph woke up he did
what the angel of the Lord had told him to do: he took his wife to
his home.*

(Matthew 1:18–24)

From this point the readings of Advent take us, step by step, through the actual
circumstances of Jesus' birth. Two of the evangelists give us accounts in their
opening chapter: Matthew, a Jew writing for Jewish converts, emphasises Jesus
as Messiah and King representing the fulfilment of God's promises to Abraham
and David. Luke, the Gentile, on the other hand stresses the universality of the
gospel message of salvation. In compiling their narratives of the birth, Matthew

writes from Joseph's standpoint, while Luke concentrates on the experience of Mary.

We begin today with Matthew: 'This is how Jesus Christ came to be born...' First of all, I think that if we want to avoid the danger of romanticising—and therefore diminishing—these familiar events, we must approach them from the utterly *human* perspective and always keep before us the dual theme that permeates them: God and humanity, God-and-us. Only then can we see that the saving power of God is complemented by the capacity of the human race to respond to it and to claim it. When we say we believe in God, we should add— and God believes in *us*! The Christmas story highlights, above all, God's tender, loving mercy and infinite patience of him who is the Kingdom awaiting the 'yes' of the human race to its final establishment.

In one respect the scriptures are the history of human response to God-with-us. In the lives of the patriarchs and prophets we have many models of what happens when a human life responds to God, and for myself I am constantly encouraged—when I read of them grappling and wrestling with a relationship with God—by the realisation that they were not divine, but *human* and as weak as we are. But then the whole of scripture reveals how God refuses the proud and raises up the humble: 'My power is made perfect in weakness' (2 Corinthians 12:9). In the same way the Gospel characters in the infancy narratives are all *ordinary* people, who become great only through their humanity and their willingness to respond to God in their lives.

We begin with Joseph, chosen by God to be head of the Holy Family. He belongs to the House of David—and in Jewish law even an adoptive son legally belongs to this line of descent—but he is what we would describe as an ordinary working-class man, a humble carpenter. But Joseph is a true son of Israel, he has a deep faith and we imagine his relationship with God must have been close. Matthew describes him as 'a man of honour', a quality borne out by his loving reaction to Mary's pregnancy (for in Deuteronomy 22 we find it is written in the law that an unmarried mother would have to be stoned to death rather than bring disgrace on the house of Israel!). Not only does Joseph have to cope with bitter disappointment, but also with the greater bombshell that was to come.

He is told in a dream to take Mary as his wife because she has conceived by the Holy Spirit. 'She will give birth to a son and *you* will call him Jesus'. (Jesus in Hebrew is Yehoshua which means 'Yahweh saves'.) 'He is the one who will save his people from their sins'. Consider the impact of this message on Joseph. In the light of the full gospel message *we* are able to relate to God through Jesus— the gentle, humble servant and shepherd as well as Lord and king; but Joseph had no such experience. For him God was Yahweh, Adonai, the LORD, so holy that he could not be named. The rituals of Jewish worship were all centred on the utter awesomeness of God. We are told that when Moses had a vision of the holiness of God in the burning bush (Exodus 3) his instinct was to fall on his knees and cover his face: his initial reaction to God's command was, 'Not *me*, I am not good enough; I'm no speaker, no one will believe me...'

Joseph, by contrast, humbly accepts. He doesn't understand but he *believes* in God's power. It's as simple as that: he believes that almighty God has chosen him to be the husband of Mary, and to be father to her son. Both responses to God are appropriate to us today. We must pray for deeper understanding of the holiness of God, so that we can spiritually fall on our knees like Moses, in wonder at who God is. But at the same time, if we believe, like Joseph, and humbly and simply surrender to God, there is no limit to what he can achieve in our own very ordinary lives.

PRAYER

O Adonai, leader of the house of Israel,
who appeared to Moses in the fire of the burning bush
and gave him the law on Sinai,
come to redeem us with an outstretched arm.

MEDITATION
Read Exodus 3:1–6

Zechariah and Elizabeth

◆◆

In the days of King Herod of Judaea there lived a priest called Zechariah... and he had a wife, Elizabeth by name, who was a descendant of Aaron. Both were worthy in the sight of God, and scrupulously observed all the commandments and observances of the Lord. But they were childless: Elizabeth was barren and they were both getting on in years.

Now it was the turn of Zechariah's section to serve, and he was exercising his priestly office before God when it fell to him by lot, as the ritual custom was, to enter the Lord's sanctuary and burn incense there. And at the hour of incense the whole congregation was outside, praying.

Then there appeared to him the angel of the Lord, standing on the right of the altar of incense. The sight disturbed Zechariah and he was overcome with fear. But the angel said to him, 'Zechariah, do not be afraid, your prayer has been heard. Your wife Elizabeth is to bear you a son and you must name him John. He will be your joy and delight and many will rejoice at his birth, for he will be great in the sight of the Lord...' Zechariah said to the angel, 'How can I be sure of this? I am an old man and my wife is getting on in years.' The angel replied, 'I am Gabriel who stands in God's presence, and I have been sent to speak to you and bring you this good news. Listen! Since you have not believed my words, which will come true at their appointed time, you will be silenced and have no power of speech until this has happened.' Meanwhile the people were waiting for Zechariah and were surprised that he stayed in the sanctuary so long. When he came out he could not speak to them, and they realised that he had received a vision in the sanctuary. But he could only make signs to them, and remained dumb...

Some time later his wife Elizabeth conceived, and for five months she kept it to herself. 'The Lord has done this for me' she said 'now that it has pleased him to take away the humiliation I suffered among men.'

(Luke 1:5–25)

Today Luke tells of the birth of John the Baptist, a story with a familiar Old Testament ring to it. It had in fact been foreshadowed several times before—a barren wife who, through the intervention of God, conceives and bears a son who will play a significant role in the destiny of Israel. Sarah gave birth to Isaac, the childless Hannah (who pleaded with God) bore the prophet Samuel, the barren wife of Manoah became the mother of Samson. Now Elizabeth, too, is to become the mother of the greatest of all the prophets.

There appears to have been nothing extraordinary about Zechariah and Elizabeth—except their faith. Barrenness in Israel meant disgrace and, inevitably, a great deal of suffering; yet these two people loved and served God in spite of their sorrow. There seems to have been no trace of bitterness or resentment; they both remained 'worthy in the sight of God'. The reward for their trust is to be great. Not only does Elizabeth bear her son, but later he is referred to by Jesus as the greatest of all children born to woman (Luke 7:28)!

What we must learn from Elizabeth and Zechariah is to 'love God anyway' and never give up hope. Sometimes we can too easily accept the things that are wrong in our lives and carry around very heavy burdens, subconsciously imagining they are beyond God's help or intervention. Yet I myself know how God can suddenly, and yes miraculously, change the circumstances of a deep problem in my life and solve it. This is what C.S. Lewis meant when he used the words 'surprised by joy'.

Zechariah had never given up hope. 'Your prayer has been answered' explained the angel Gabriel. To think that though they were both old and apparently long past having children, they had not given up praying! Yet poor Zechariah, having done all that, at the moment of being surprised by joy he actually couldn't believe it. All his life he has declared his belief in almighty God but when it came to God showing himself almighty, he asks for a sign and is struck dumb in consequence. It is an eminently human reaction (would we, if we were suddenly visited by the angel Gabriel, grasp at once that God would do the impossible in our lives?). But herein is the lesson of this episode, and indeed of the whole season of Advent: *nothing is impossible to God*. We cannot limit God by the restrictions of our own human understanding: if we do that we're simply not letting him be God. The mystery of God *is* beyond us, all we can do is be open enough to receive him on his terms. Then we can join with Elizabeth in exclaiming, 'The Lord has done this for me!'

As we prepare, finally, to meditate on the prayer for today, we can draw a parallel between Elizabeth, old in years yet bearing new life within her, and Israel itself, worn and weary yet about to bring forth a new 'shoot springing from the stock of Jesse', as Isaiah had predicted 800 years earlier; 'on him the spirit of the Lord rests' (11:1–2). Thus are the old and new covenants inseparably bound together, and we must pray all the more earnestly for reconciliation between root and branch, Jew and Gentile.

PRAYER
O come, shoot of Jesse,
who stands as an ensign for the people,
before whom kings shall shut their mouths,
whom the Gentiles shall seek after,
come to deliver us.
Delay now no longer.

MEDITATION
Read Luke 1:5–25

The Annunciation ADVENT 4/TUESDAY

◆◆

*In the sixth month the angel Gabriel was sent by God to a town
in Galilee called Nazareth, to a virgin betrothed to a man named
Joseph, of the House of David; and the virgin's name was Mary.
He went in and said to her, 'Rejoice, so highly favoured! The Lord
is with you.'*

*She was deeply disturbed by these words and asked herself what
this greeting could mean, but the angel said to her, 'Mary, do not
be afraid; you have won God's favour. Listen! You are to conceive
and bear a son, and you must name him Jesus. He will be great
and will be called Son of the Most High. The Lord God will give
him the throne of his ancestor David; he will rule over the House
of Jacob for ever and his reign will have no end.'*

*Mary said to the angel, 'But how can this come about, since I
am a virgin?'*

*'The Holy Spirit will come upon you' the angel answered 'and
the power of the Most High will cover you with its shadow. And so
the child will be holy and will be called Son of God. Know this
too: your kinswoman Elizabeth has, in her old age, herself
conceived a son, and she whom people called barren is now in her
sixth month, for nothing is impossible to God.'*

*'I am the handmaid of the Lord,' said Mary 'let what you have
said be done to me.' And the angel left her.*

(Luke 1:26–38)

In today's famous Advent reading we are given an account of the event which
turned the course of history: Mary's 'yes' to God which would make it possible
for God to become man and, by assuming that same human nature that was
overcome by Evil in the Garden of Eden, to overcome Evil himself. Because of
one human life surrendered to God freely and simply, the door to the salvation
of mankind will be opened. St Bernard of Clairvaux, in one of his homilies on
this reading, paints a picture of the whole human race kneeling in the valley of
the shadow of death, begging Mary to say yes. 'Answer, O virgin, answer speedily.
Speak the word and receive the word, offer what is yours, conceive what is of
God. Give what is temporal and embrace what is eternal… Behold the desired

of all nations is outside knocking at your door. Arise, then run and open!'

Mary is a supremely great figure, but I think we diminish her greatness if we make her into someone 'special' and fail to recognise that she is, first and foremost, an ordinary human being from an ordinary little town which was (and still is) the back of beyond. 'From Nazareth!' exclaimed Nathaniel later on in John's Gospel. 'Can anything good come from that place?' It was with the same tone of voice that an Israeli passenger next to me on a flight to the Holy Land described Nazareth to me (I understood when I got there what he meant: it is drab and seedy!). Yet this young Jewish girl who lived there is addressed by the angel more impressively than any other person in the Bible, *'so highly favoured'*.

This salutation surely tells us that in this ordinary life there must have been great faith in her God—and any shred of doubt is dispelled by her response. Mystified, uncomprehending, she does not demur or protest like others before her had. Moses had said, Send anyone but me! Gideon said, I'm weak, you'll have to give me some kind of sign. Isaiah said, Woe is me, I'm wretched! Jeremiah said, But I'm too young. Zechariah said, My wife is too old. And who can't sympathise with them? It's easier to believe God can work miracles in other people—but in ourselves...?

But listen to Mary's response, a virgin who's just been told she's going to conceive a child: she just says 'How?' No ifs or buts, no worrying about the past or future, simply 'How are you going to do it?' Unlike the rest of us who put such limits on God in our lives, she understands the greatness of God and believes his power can transform her ordinary human life. Thus she is the first human being to hear the salvation message of the gospel, and her response is 'Be it done unto me according to your word'.

Not only is she the mother of the Messiah, she is also the first disciple. There are few enough references to her in the rest of the Gospel texts, but sufficient to teach us that in the spiritual life we don't have to understand everything before we say 'yes'. Mary did not understand Simeon's prophecy ('this child will reveal the secret thoughts of men's hearts... and a sword will pierce your own heart'); neither she nor Joseph understood Jesus staying in the Temple (Luke 2). Mary had to follow Jesus like the other disciples and learn the teaching of the gospel at his feet. She had no extra status as mother during the public ministry of her son—in answer to the woman who cried out 'Happy is the womb that bore you', Jesus said 'but still happier are those who hear the word of God and keep it' (Luke 11:27–28).

Though highly favoured of God Mary still had to hear the word of God and keep it, and as disciple go the whole way with God right up to the point of

Calvary, from the joy of new birth to the sorrow of the cross and the glory of the resurrection. (At the foot of the cross Mary was honoured by the dying Jesus with an even more significant motherhood—she became mother of disciples, when Jesus enjoined his beloved disciple to 'behold thy mother'.)

Perhaps the most important lesson we can learn from her model of discipleship, in our own efforts to follow Jesus, is that when she didn't understand she *pondered everything in her heart*, which is a simple but concise definition of prayer. Prayer is simply pondering the mystery of God, sitting at the feet of Jesus and quietly pondering his words, gradually allowing God to reveal himself through the Gospels. Let us pray today that, just as Mary's 'yes' opened the door for the salvation of the world, a new door to deeper faith and commitment may be opened for us; and at the same time pray for those in our world who sit in darkness and unbelief. May we become a light for them. Like Mary, let us arise, run and open.

PRAYER
O come, key of David
and sceptre of the house of Israel.
You open a door that no man can shut,
you close a door that no man can open.
Come and bring bound out of the dungeon
him who is sitting in darkness
and in the shadow of death.

MEDITATION
Meditate quietly and slowly on the above passage.

Shout for joy! ADVENT 4/WEDNESDAY

◆◆

Shout for joy, daughter of Zion,
Israel, shout aloud!
Rejoice, exult with all your heart,
daughter of Jerusalem!
The Lord has repealed your sentence;
he has driven your enemies away.
The Lord, the king of Israel, is in your midst;
you have no more evil to fear.
When that day comes, word will come to Jerusalem:
Zion, have no fear,
do not let your hands fall limp.
The Lord your God is in your midst,
a victorious warrior.
He will exult with joy over you,
he will renew you by his love;
he will dance with shouts of joy for you
as on a day of festival.

(Zephaniah 3:14–18)

Today the commercial world will be reminding us that we have only 'x' shopping days to Christmas. Go to any shopping-centre and you will find an air of single-mindedness, everyone stepping out just a few paces quicker; no idle passing of the time, just a determination to get all that is required to celebrate in a fitting manner.

Spiritually we need the same kind of determination, to approach Christmas Day with a desire to receive all it has to offer! We may recall Elizabeth's words to Mary: 'Blessed are you because you have believed God's promise to you will be fulfilled' (Luke 1:45). Mary's own joy is mirrored by a friend with a similar experience, and together they suddenly grasp the reality of God's miracle. The scene always reminds me of a single log smouldering away on a fire; put another log alongside it and the two catch fire and the flames leap and roar. So Mary and Elizabeth, in their experience with God, are on fire with joy.

This is what we, too, are called upon to experience: what happened to Mary can happen to us. It is not something we can achieve, but something we receive if we are open enough to receive it. Wherever we are in our walk with God, frail sinners not saints, we must stretch out our empty hands and pray that God will dwell anew deep within us. 'Have no fear', says the prophet above, 'do not let your hands grow limp. The Lord your God is in *you* . . .'

In the words of our prayer for today we are all in darkness of a kind, prisoners of problems that we might be aware of or that may be too painful to face. There are those who are crippled with jealousy or possessiveness; those who are nursing a deep anger. There are some whose hidden stresses manifest themselves in physical disease, others so fearful that every ache and pain seems bound to be fatal. There are those afflicted with fears and terrible pessimism, seeing disaster at every turn; and those who crave for acceptance (because they have not learned to accept themselves) and then suffer agonies of rejection. And most demoralised of all, there are those paralysed by recurring depression . . . the list is endless of course.

But God did promise us that the Messiah would resurrect his people from darkness. 'The glory of the Lord is rising on you, though night still covers the earth and darkness the peoples. Above you the Lord now rises and above you his glory appears' (Isaiah 60:1–2). And later on he will 'bind up hearts that are broken, proclaim liberty to captives, freedom to those in prison . . .' (61:1). It may seem more comfortable for people with apparently insoluble problems to stay in hiding under cover of darkness, but if we are too afraid to emerge then we are refusing to let this glorious light shine on our dark areas and bring healing and wholeness.

As the season reaches its climax let us gather together all the images and teachings of Advent and convert them into a personal reality: above all, to understand our individual need of God and to cry out to him, Come, come and rescue *me*! We must approach Christmas with our sights set high. We *weren't* created to crawl in the dust with the serpent (Genesis 3), but to soar like eagles to the very highest places. This is why God became man, to overcome darkness, and turn our mourning into dancing, our sorrow into joy.

PRAYER
O rising sun,
you are the splendour of eternal light,
and the sun of justice.
O come, and enlighten those who sit
in darkness and the shadow of death.

MEDITATION
Read Isaiah 61:1–4

The Magnificat

♦♦

'My soul proclaims the greatness of the Lord
and my spirit exults in God my saviour;
because he has looked upon his lowly handmaid.
Yes, from this day forward all generations will
*   call me blessed,*
for the Almighty has done great things for me.
Holy is his name,
and his mercy reaches from age to age for those
*   who fear him.*
He has shown the power of his arm,
he has routed the proud heart.
He has pulled down princes from their thrones and
*   exalted the lowly.*
The hungry he has filled with good things, the rich
*   sent empty away.*
He has come to the help of Israel his servant,
*   mindful of his mercy—*
according to the promise he made to our ancestors—
of his mercy to Abraham and to his descendants for ever!'

(Luke 1:46–55)

In all the two thousand years since the birth of Jesus his followers have never ceased to pray to God the Father through him and in his Holy Spirit. Prayer—the communicating of love between God and creature—*can* penetrate the darkness and reach out to a suffering world. Now we only see through a glass darkly (as St Paul says) but who knows what will finally have been accomplished by prayer? Perhaps the worn-out mother snatching a few precious moments with God, or perhaps the professional (as it were) in a monastery detailed to a hour of prayer yet feeling dry and uninspired—they may think their offering of prayer paltry. Yet they may have tapped the unlimited source of God's power by their simple willingness, and given the world more than they could ever dream of.

Marx claimed that religion was the opium of the people but if Communism ever achieved its goal—the elimination of religion—it would only have destroyed institutions and hierarchies. It would not, and could not, touch the continuing prayer-life of the Church, which would remain rock-like. The Church, after all, is not bricks and mortar; it is the hearts of people, and in their hearts the capacity for loving is fired through prayer. I think of it as a school for loving—by drawing on God's love, our horizons are infinitely widened and the range of our love becomes universal.

The Magnificat, Mary's famous prayer, has held a central place in Christian worship through the centuries: it has been recited at evening prayer, monks have chanted it, composers in every age set it to music. Magnificat! Thus is the greatness of God proclaimed in perpetuity, his promises assured, his ways made known! It is, above all, an affirmation, the prayer of one who 'knows'. It is a prayer of exultant joy, yes, but also one of quiet serenity: 'Now I see, now I understand'. It is in knowing God like that the spiritual journey moves from the foothills to scaling the summit.

If I may be allowed a personal interpretation here. I like to think that after the Annunciation Mary believed in what God could do and agreed to surrender herself, but when God provided her with a friend with a similar experience suddenly everything was confirmed. Belief blossomed into certainty. They both 'knew'. And this is our destination too. We worship, we believe, we ask and we seek and, if we're really serious, we pray and allow the word of God to become alive and active in us. Thereby we will be relating one-to-one with God—the most important relationship we will ever have.

If we learn to pray through the Gospels, letting them really speak to us, we can acquire the first essential for spiritual growth: that is, to 'know' Jesus. He himself said 'learn from me' (Matthew 11:29). Of course we will encounter trials and testing (like Mary) and doubtless we will fail over and over again. But, as the Letter to the Hebrews puts it, we must 'keep running steadily in the race', straining for the prize ahead, which is the utter certainty of the Magnificat. When I know the greatness of God in the deepest centre of my being, then my spirit will rejoice. Then I will understand his absolute holiness, his loving forgiveness, his faithfulness to his promises to every generation right up to the present day. Then he will work marvels in my life. Holy is his name!

PRAYER

O King, whom all the people desire,
you are the corner-stone
which makes all one.
O come and save!

MEDITATION

Read 1 Samuel 2:1, 4–8

Confession

◆◆◆

[The Lord God says this:] Look, I am going to send my messenger
to prepare a way before me... Know that I am going to send you
Elijah the prophet before my day comes... He shall turn the
hearts of fathers towards their children and the hearts of children
towards their fathers.

(Malachi 3:1, 4:5–6[3:23–24])

Happy is the man whose offence is forgiven,
whose sin is remitted.
O happy the man to whom the Lord
imputes no guilt,
in whose spirit is no guile.
I kept it secret and my frame was wasted.
I groaned all the day long
for night and day your hand
was heavy upon me.
Indeed, my strength was dried up
as by the summer's heat.
But now I have acknowledged my sins;
my guilt I did not hide.
I said: 'I will confess
my offence to the Lord.'
And you, Lord, have forgiven
the guilt of my sin.

(Psalm 32[31]:1–5)

In today's reading from Malachi we are once again reminded of the new
Elijah—John the Baptist, who like his predecessor preached the message of
preparation. And appropriately, just as we are prompted to return to the theme
of repentance at the beginning of the season of Advent, so we are as it draws to
its climax.

The Greek word for repentance could strictly be translated as 'change of mind' and any spiritual journey has to involve continual change. We must be constantly challenged to move on or else we become stunted. There is a most vivid metaphor of this in the two famous seas of Israel. The Sea of Galilee, which receives constant replenishment from the Jordan, teems with life and provides food for all who live close by. By contrast the Dead Sea has only desultory inlets and no outlet: it has no movement, it is heavy and lifeless. With the sun sparkling on the surface it is pleasant enough to look at, yet it is sinister in its deadness.

If Advent is going to be any kind of turning point for us, we must be prepared to examine ourselves and see what it is that blocks *our* movement, our growth. In this kind of self-scrutiny, I believe it is helpful to understand the nature of God as a loving Father. A loving father disciplines his children *because* he loves them, and it is a simple fact that an undisciplined child will have a far more difficult passage through life than one who has been lovingly disciplined. A loving father must train his child to cope with life and, as the writer of the Letter to the Hebrews reminds us, ' "the Lord trains the ones he loves"... but he does it all for our own good, so that we may share his own holiness' (12:6, 10).

It follows, therefore, that our response must be 'like little children'; and we must in fact learn a lesson from how small children react to discipline. A parent seeing a child doing something dangerous will scold it: there might be a few tears, but if the child trusts the parent it will understand, obey and soon forget the tears. The more complex adult mind has an extra problem to cope with, and that is guilt. If we respond to any discipline with guilt, we will never enjoy that freedom which is the fruit of true repentance. A truly repentant sinner responds to forgiveness with joy, like the psalmist: 'The Lord listened and had pity. The Lord came to my help. [He] changed my mourning into dancing' (30[29])! False guilt arises from a misunderstanding of God's forgiveness, from the pride of not being able to face up to being wrong. Facing up to and confessing our sins—to one another, to a priest, or to God—is to be set free of the false (or real) burden of guilt. If, as our psalm for today puts it, we keep it secret we will carry the weight of it 'groaning all the day long'.

If false guilt is a block to spiritual progress, so too I think is false forgiveness. We are also called to forgive others, but if when we have gone through all the motions of forgiveness, said and done all the right things, there still lurks a hidden resentment, then that is no forgiveness. To forgive and not forget is not possible: real forgiveness always forgets. If we keep coming back to it, then it's we who need help. And if we fall at the feet of Jesus and admit we need help, it is then the channel of grace is opened up.

Of course there are other obstacles to progress, pride, self-centredness, lack of love... I think it is very helpful in this respect to read Galatians 5:16–26 slowly and prayerfully, for a kind of spiritual checklist. And if I can share one of my own problems: for years I thought one of my main failings was my tongue and I often prayed the psalmist's prayer, 'Lord, set a guard over my mouth' (141[140]:3). But then I came across the passage in the Gospels where Jesus says: 'A man's words flow out of what fills his heart' (Matthew 15:18). It was then I realised my problem went a lot deeper than my tongue!

Whatever it is that blocks our progress, there is hope for all of us. We begin our journey to Bethlehem with empty hands and heavy loads, but we can travel secure in the conviction that if our hearts and minds are open to him, God *will* come and save us. Immanuel will come.

PRAYER

*O Immanuel, you are our king
and our judge,
the one whom the people await.
O come, and save us, Lord our God*

The Light of the World CHRISTMAS EVE

●●

The people that walked in darkness
has seen a great light;
on those who live in a land of deep shadow
a light has shone.
You have made their gladness greater,
you have made their joy increase;
they rejoice in your presence
as men rejoice at harvest time,
as men are happy when they are dividing
the spoils.
For the yoke that was weighing on him,
the bar across his shoulders,
the rod of his oppressor,
these you break as on the day of Midian...
For there is a child born for us,
a son given to us
and dominion is laid on his shoulders;
and this is the name they give him:
Wonder-Counsellor, Mighty-God,
Eternal-Father, Prince-of-Peace.

(Isaiah 9:2–6)

*C*hristmas Eve (evening) Sometimes, at this time on Christmas Eve, I find myself recalling some lines from Shakespeare—the scene on the battlements at Elsinore:

Some say, that ever 'gainst that season comes
Wherein our Saviour's birth is celebrated,
The bird of dawning singeth all night long:
And then, they say, no spirit can walk abroad;
The nights are wholesome; then no planets strike
No fairy takes, nor witch hath power to charm,
So hallow'd and so gracious is the time.

Hamlet I. i. 158–164

For me it captures the magic tranquillity of the moment, the peacefulness. I only recently discovered that, historically, at the time of Christ's birth, the world (that is to say, the Roman world) *was* at peace. The earlier civil wars had been resolved and the frontiers, including Judaea, were settled for a time. The gates of the temple of Mars in the Forum at Rome were closed, apparently for the first and last time. 'How silently, how silently, the wondrous gift is given.' The Prince of Peace born in an interlude when there was peace on earth.

To experience the wonder of this holy night we need to take time to be silent and alone. I still remember, as a small child, on Christmas Eve when everyone else seemed preoccupied, stealing away to the room where the Christmas tree was. I would turn out the room lights and just sit staring at the tree shimmering and sparkling with jewelled lights, letting my eyes feast on the beauty of it all. With the passing years the initial wonder of the Christmas tree has faded a little perhaps, but the marvel of faith has increased and I still feel the need to go somewhere quiet and silently feast on the wonder of this holy night. Sometimes it might be outside in the frosty night, just gazing at the (hopefully clear and starry) sky, pondering the mystery of what took place in Bethlehem 2,000 years ago. The thoughts are always the same: How can it be? How could almighty God actually become man—one of us? Yet we dare to believe it. This is our faith. This is the divine exchange, Jesus humbling himself to share in our humanity in order that we may share his divinity. We can only confess with the psalmist that 'such knowledge is beyond my understanding, a height to which my mind cannot attain' (139[138]:6).

*C*hristmas Eve (midnight) When Mary brought forth her son there was no royal fanfare, no 21-gun salute, no balcony announcement to the waiting throng, no flash-bulbs, TV cameramen or teleprinter messages. Outside the stable the crowds in Bethlehem went about their business, unaware that anything momentous was happening other than the census that had brought them there in the first place. But heaven was celebrating the birthday of life, life for all mankind. 'And suddenly with the angel there was a great throng of the heavenly host, praising God and singing: "Glory to God in the highest... and peace to men"' (Luke 2:13–14).

Significantly the only ones to whom this was communicated were the shepherds, quiet in the fields outside the village. Modern theologians may make light of the shepherds, but for me they symbolise the poor in spirit, those humble enough to seek and find God in our mundane human circumstances: they gazed into the clear and starry night and *saw* the light. We should, like the shepherds, be humble enough to seek the Christ child and kneel before the manger with nothing to offer but the poverty of being human. Our lives we *can* offer; we can pray, 'Come and rescue me and redeem the whole of my life so that I may join the heavenly throng and see the vision of your glory'. We can join the angels and cry: 'Glory to God in the highest, and peace to all men'.

PRAYER

O come, all ye faithful,
joyful and triumphant.
O come to Bethlehem.
Come and behold him, born the king of angels.
Come, let us adore him, Christ the Lord.

The Season of Christmas

The Word made flesh CHRISTMAS DAY

◆◆

> *At various times in the past and in various different ways, God*
> *spoke to our ancestors through the prophets; but in our own time,*
> *the last days, he has spoken to us through his Son, the Son that*
> *he has appointed to inherit everything and through whom he*
> *made everything there is. He is the radiant light of God's glory*
> *and the perfect copy of his nature, sustaining the universe by his*
> *powerful command; and now that he has destroyed the defilement*
> *of sin, he has gone to take his place in heaven at the right hand of*
> *divine Majesty. So he is now as far above the angels as the title*
> *which he has inherited is higher than their own name.*
>
> *(Hebrews 1:1–4)*

Today is a great feast day; today we feast, both spiritually and in a material sense, in celebration of the Word made flesh, Jesus who described himself as 'the bread of life'. (How appropriate, by the way, that he was born in Bethlehem which literally translated means 'house of bread'!)

In the Jewish calendar feasts were a central element of worship. Our own eucharistic feast can be linked historically with the offerings of the firstfruits of man's labour at God's altar, as described in Deuteronomy: 'You must lay them [the firstfruits] before the Lord your God, and bow down in the sight of the Lord your God. Then you are to feast on all the good things the Lord has given you, you and your household... and the stranger who lives among you' (26:10–11). In this foreshadowing of the eucharist the first of the harvest and the firstborn animals were taken to the altar to be sanctified, these parts representing the whole. When the people shared the consecrated food they in turn became consecrated and symbolically represented the whole of humanity. In this letter St James applies this to the Christian Church: 'By his own choice he made us his children by the message of the truth so that we should be a sort of first-fruits of all that he had created' (1:18).

Today is the day when Jesus became the firstborn son, the new Adam, the firstfruit of humanity fulfilling the ancient law. On Calvary he will become the sacrificial lamb, consecrating us. He is the word made flesh: no longer (as our reading underlines) does God speak through patriarchs and prophets, but directly through Jesus to us. 'It is the only Son' to quite John's beautiful Gospel prologue, 'who is nearest to the Father's heart, who has made him known'. But, on this feast of feasts, we recall that Jesus himself told us, 'I am the bread of life'. Whoever comes to him will never be hungry, whoever believes in him will not thirst. 'I am the *living* bread which has come down from heaven. Anyone who eats this bread will live for ever; and the bread that I shall give is my flesh, for the life of the world' (John 6:35–51).

At the time some of Jesus' audience thought that he was referring to the manna from heaven, sent to the Israelites on their exodus—which indirectly he was. But I wonder if they had also recalled the tradition, from the Book of Wisdom, which described manna as 'satisfying every taste. And the substance you gave demonstrated your sweetness towards your children, for, conforming to the taste of whoever ate it, it transformed itself into what each eater wished' (16:20–21). In retrospect we can take up the analogy: Jesus represents the sweetness of God towards his children. He can also transform himself into what we need. If we expect much of him, we will be given much. 'To him who has, more will be given' (Matthew 25:29). And elsewhere: 'Blessed are they who hunger and thirst after righteousness, they will have their fill' (Matthew 5:6).

Today we can feast richly on the fruits of the earth. Let us at the same time pray for the will to feast as well on the riches of heaven, to taste the sweetness of God who alone can satisfy our deepest hunger.

PRAYER

Wisdom has built herself a house,
she has erected her seven pillars,
she has slaughtered her beasts, prepared her wine,
she has laid her table.
She has despatched her maidservants
and proclaimed from the city's heights:
'Who is ignorant? Let him step this way.'
To the fool she says,
'Come and eat my bread,
drink the wine I have prepared!
Leave your folly and you will live,
walk in the ways of perception.'

(Proverbs 9:1–6)

MEDITATION

Read John 1:1–8

Love your enemies

◆◆

*Stephen was filled with grace and power and began to work
miracles and great signs among the people. But then certain
people came forward to debate with Stephen, some from Cyrene
and Alexandria who were members of the synagogue called the
Synagogue of Freedmen, and others from Cilicia and Asia. They
found they could not get the better of him because of his wisdom,
and because it was the Spirit that prompted what he said...*

*[Later, members of the Sanhedrin] were infuriated when they
heard... and ground their teeth at him. But Stephen, filled with
the Holy Spirit, gazed into heaven and saw the glory of God, and
Jesus standing at God's right hand. 'I can see heaven thrown
open' he said 'and the Son of Man standing at the right hand of
God.' At this all the members of the council shouted out and
stopped their ears with their hands; then they all rushed at him,
sent him out of the city and stoned him. The witnesses put down
their clothes at the feet of a young man called Saul. As they were
stoning him, Stephen said in invocation, 'Lord Jesus, receive my
spirit'. Then he knelt down and said aloud, 'Lord, do not hold
this sin against them'; and with these words he fell asleep. Saul
entirely approved of the killing.*

(Acts of the Apostles 6:8–10, 7:54—8:1)

After we have shared in the joy of the birth of Jesus, we now look forward to
the birth of a new age—and with it the new commandment Jesus himself laid
upon us: 'Love one another, as I have loved you'. And the ultimate criterion of
this love, we are told, is 'greater love has no man than that he would lay down
his life for his friends' (John 15:12–13). By this yardstick Stephen was the first
disciple to become a full witness to how the love of Christ can transform a
human being into his own likeness.

Stephen, whose martyrdom we commemorate today, had received the Holy
Spirit, probably at Pentecost: he was so inspired by the love of God that, like
Jesus, he was able to say of his enemies, 'Father, forgive them', even as they put

him to death. Such love cannot but bear fruit—and, as we know, one of the greatest Christian witnesses.

All through the New Testament, when people were confronted with the truth of the gospel message they displayed one of three reactions: there was a positive response, there was indifference, and then sometimes there was fear. And fear triggered off the most primitive of all instincts, the instinct to destroy. In the two thousand years or so since Stephen, little has changed but the means of destroying: succeeding generations have produced their martyrs, shining witnesses to the love of God that overcomes all evil. We are 'surrounded by a cloud of witnesses' (Hebrews 12:1) on all sides and in every age.

That includes, sadly, our own age. Today the authoritarian response is 'kill it'; and there are still Christians who suffer torture, imprisonment and death (even though the lesson of all history is that religion is not overcome by persecution, but rather flourishes under it!). In 1991 we were powerfully and movingly reminded of them, when the Pope and the Archbishop of Canterbury knelt together in prayer before seven candlesticks representing seven modern Christian martyrs: Martin Luther King, the civil rights leader; Dietrich Bonhoeffer, who was executed for his opposition to the Nazis; Maximilian Kolbe who gave his life in exchange for a Jew in a concentration camp; Archbishop Oscar Romero, gunned down in San Salvador while celebrating Mass; Bishop Janani Luwum, put to death under Idi Amin's brutal regime; and Maria Skobtsova, the Russian Orthodox nun who died in Ravensbruk. The seventh candlestick stood for the 'unknown martyr', the legion of people who sacrificed themselves but whose names we do not—and probably never will—know.

If *we* are to follow Jesus we must, through the working of the Holy Spirit, become like him. Impossible, we think. Not me, I'm no saint. Yet we must learn from Mary: not to say 'No', but 'How?'—and to understand that his power can overshadow our feeble lives too, because nothing is impossible to God. Today we pray for all persecuted Christians, and ask for ourselves the gift of love, a love which is not afraid to stand up and oppose the world's prevailing dogmas and ideologies.

PRAYER

Into your hands I commend my spirit.
It is you who will redeem me, Lord...
As for me, I trust in the Lord:
let me be glad and rejoice in your love...
My life is in your hands, deliver me
from the hands of those who hate me.
Let your face shine on your servant.
Save me in your love.

(Psalm 31[30]:5–6, 15–16)

MEDITATION
Read Matthew 10:17–22

The beloved disciple

◆◆

Something which has existed since the beginning,
that we have heard,
and we have seen with our own eyes;
that we have watched
and touched with our own hands:
the Word, who is life—
this is our subject.
That life was made visible:
we saw it and we are giving our testimony,
telling you of the eternal life
which was with the Father and has been made
visible to us.
What we have seen and heard
we are telling you
so that you too may be in union with us,
as we are in union
with the Father
and with his Son Jesus Christ.
We are writing this to you to make our own joy
complete.

(1 John 1:1–4)

Today's reading is taken from the first letter of 'John', the apostolic figure who in the Fourth Gospel appears as Jesus' 'beloved disciple'. I see John as one of that body of witnesses who, through the history of Christianity, have been so powerfully bound up with God that they have become spiritual lovers, people who fall in love with God. Like Mary (the sister of Martha) who simply sits at the feet of Jesus listening to his words, content just to be in his presence, so John seemed to have a vocation of love—leaning on the breast of Jesus, loving him purely and simply.

In his Gospel John does not merely report scenes and incidents: it is not so much a record of what Jesus said and did, but a deep reflection on the significance of those events and on what Jesus *meant* by what he said. John is first and foremost a witness to the word of God: the opening phrase of his prologue echoes the very first words of the Bible, 'In the beginning God created...' By his spoken word God created the world; now the word is flesh and dwelling among us, and *we saw* his glory'. And this is the underlying emphasis of all John's writing: he did not see Jesus as the suffering servant of Mark's Gospel, or the Davidic king of Matthew, or even the universal Son of Man as Luke did. What John sees is God incarnate on earth, transcendent, glorious!

John is a disciple who 'knows' from first-hand. Jesus was someone he had personally seen, heard, watched, touched and, thanks be to God, his witness is still alive for us today and continues to speak to us of the glory of God. He was, as we know, one of the trio of Jesus' closest disciples (Peter, James and John), and we can learn much from what was written about him and what he himself recorded in his own Gospel. While Peter for instance was destined to be a great leader, the heart of John's witness is *personal relationship* with Jesus and God. His vocation is bound up in the first commandment, loving God above all, staying close. In the Gospels he is always there—in the high priest's palace at the time of the trial (while Peter stays outside) (John 18:15), at the foot of the cross with Mary (19:26), and he is the first to believe in the resurrection (20:8).

The point is that, because God is number one in John's life, he ends up as the most forceful evangelist of all. Perhaps that tells us that beloved disciples, those whose lives are built on prayer, who stay close to God in an attentive, reflective relationship, have more to offer the world than the achievers, because they are the ones who 'know' God and are utterly certain of his power and glory. (I am reminded here of one of the modern leading evangelists, who confessed at a world evangelical conference that if he lived his life over again he would spend less time preaching, and more time praying.) John offers us the complete recipe for loving God. If we require teaching on prayer and ministry, we need look no further than John 15: read it slowly and prayerfully, allowing it to speak to your heart.

PRAYER

God of hosts, turn again, we implore,
look down from heaven and see.
Visit this vine and protect it,
the vine your right hand has planted.

(Psalm 80[79]:14–15)

MEDITATION

Read John 20:2–8

Holy Innocents

◆◆

After they had left, the angel of the Lord appeared to Joseph in a dream and said, 'Get up, take the child and his mother with you, and escape into Egypt, and stay there until I tell you, because Herod intends to search for the child and do away with him'. So Joseph got up and, taking the child and his mother with him, left that night for Egypt, where he stayed until Herod was dead. This was to fulfil what the Lord had spoken through the prophet: 'I called my son out of Egypt'. Herod was furious when he realised that he had been outwitted by the wise men, and in Bethlehem and its surrounding district he had all the male children killed who were two years old or under, reckoning by the date he had been careful to ask the wise men. It was then that the words spoken through the prophet Jeremiah were fulfilled: 'A voice was heard in Ramah, sobbing and loudly lamenting: it was Rachel weeping for her children, refusing to be comforted because they were no more'.

(Matthew 2:13–18)

Today's text makes sombre reading, but it does remind us of the ever-present 'enemy', of the spiritual war that St Paul describes in Ephesians (6:10–20). The Bible begins with conflict—'I will make you enemies of each other, you and the woman, your offspring and her offspring' (Genesis 3:15)—though the precise origin and nature of man's enemy is a mystery. Man's capacity to become eternal and share in the divine nature of God has been, and still is, threatened by the enemy 'striking the heel' of his people.

Throughout the Old Testament God's people suffered persecution, but the ultimate message was that God's power is always greater and that his people were destined to bring forth the Messiah. One of the earliest manifestations of the enemy was Pharaoh in the Book of Exodus, who dreadfully presages Herod's solution by exterminating all the male Hebrew children. But God (who never needs large majorities) in that case worked through a single Hebrew woman hiding her child and trusting his life to God in a basket on the Nile. This child would eventually rescue his people from the domination of the enemy—an historical preface to the spiritual exodus when Jesus would lead his people from death to life.

At the birth of Jesus the enemy was still in evidence, thwarted this time by Joseph's faith and obedience. In due course 'at the appointed time' the enemy does succeed in putting Jesus to death, but it is precisely in this horrific death—in the depths of human ignominy and at the limits of human suffering—that the enemy is confronted and confounded by incarnate love. 'Father, forgive them' (Luke 23:34). And throughout the ages men and women have continued to confound the enemy by laying down their lives, as their Lord did before them (the blood of the martyrs, it is said, is the seed of the Church).

The conflict continues in our own time—atrocities such as perhaps even Pharaoh or Herod never dreamed of, such as the extermination of six million Jews. Communism, openly opposed to all religion, infiltrates societies and nurtures revolution, breeding counter-revolution and more violence and death. Vietnam, Africa and Central America where bodies are swept into heaps on the side of the road and dumped in mass graves. Yet how can *we* respond to this catalogue of the work of the enemy that is flashed onto our TV screens night after night? The answer is that we must take up the challenge at a personal level, and never underestimate what the faith of one person can accomplish, whether it is a Hebrew midwife or a Jewish carpenter. Jesus warned his disciples (John 16:33) that they would have trouble in this world. But he went on to exhort them, 'Be brave, I have conquered the world.' 'I am the way, the truth and the life' (John 14:6).

Our response must be to follow this way, whatever the consequences. If you imagine a pair of weighing scales balanced with an equal amount of good and evil, perhaps my life, my decision, may be the one that tips the balance! If I am receiving light and life in a darkened world, then I am able to give light and life to others. And when enough people simply and sincerely turn to God in the depths of their hearts to plead for his kingdom to come, it *will*!

PRAYER

Lord, may your kingdom come.
May your will be done
on earth as it is in heaven.

MEDITATION
Read Revelation 21:1–4

Simeon

◆◆

When the day came for them to be purified as laid down by the Law of Moses, [the parents of Jesus] took him up to Jerusalem to present him to the Lord—observing what stands written in the Law of the Lord: 'Every first-born male must be consecrated to the Lord'—and also to offer in sacrifice, in accordance with what is said in the Law of the Lord, 'a pair of turtledoves or two young pigeons'. Now in Jerusalem there was a man named Simeon. He was an upright and devout man; he looked forward to Israel's comforting and the Holy Spirit rested on him. It had been revealed to him by the Holy Spirit that he would not see death until he had set eyes on the Christ of the Lord. Prompted by the Spirit he came to the Temple: and when the parents brought in the child Jesus to do for him what the Law required, he took him into his arms and blessed God; and he said:
'Now, Master, you can let your servant go in peace,
just as you promised;
because my eyes have seen the salvation
which you have prepared for all the nations to see,
a light to enlighten the pagans
and the glory of your people Israel'.

As the child's father and mother stood there wondering at the things that were being said about him, Simeon blessed them and said to Mary his mother, 'You see this child: he is destined for the fall and for the rising of many in Israel, destined to be a sign that is rejected—and a sword will pierce your own soul too—so that the secret thoughts of many may be laid bare'.

(Luke 2:22–35)

In Simeon I think we have a beautiful example of a life given to God. Clearly here is a man with a close relationship with God in prayer, close enough for the Holy Spirit to confer on him a promise of the fulfilment of all his aspirations (even in this life, it strikes me, God chooses to bless his intimate friends with the realisation of their hopes and desires). Simeon is a marvellous lesson in 'hope'—that is, of setting one's sights high and having the faith to expect great things from God.

And God *does* fulfil his promises: not with a fanfare of trumpets but in the normal course of everyday life. Doubtless for Simeon it started off as a routine sort of day in this noisy, bustling city of trade and pilgrimage. Perhaps the gentle prompting to go to the Temple was interpreted at first as a call to an hour or so's prayer and worship. But Simeon's spiritual eyes were open and, in the infant Jesus, his love of God and his hope for his people were rewarded with the full light of revelation. Outwardly there could have been nothing about the slightly bewildered parents, obviously poor (pigeons were traditionally the offering of the poor) and routinely carrying out the requirements of the Law, to single them out. But the note of certainty in the old man's song of thanksgiving (the Nunc Dimittis which is still recited, appropriately enough, at the end of each day) is unmistakable.

Note that Simeon, although a devout and orthodox Jew, 'looking forward to Israel's comforting', nevertheless predicts the salvation of *all* nations, not just of his own. Note, too, that his prophecy foretells the threefold pattern of man's redemption—from joy to sorrow to glory. This child will be a sign that is rejected, and Mary will share the pain of that rejection as a witness to her son's passion and death. But through these events the nature of man's true quest for God will be exposed: there will be no more pretence; man can either believe in God's only Son and come into the light of full revelation, or else refuse and remain in the darkness of unbelief. This is the sword of division that Jesus himself later spoke of, the division between belief and unbelief: 'On these grounds is sentence pronounced: that though the light has come into the world, men have shown they prefer darkness to the light' (John 3:19).

Today we ask to be like Simeon; we ask for the insight to find the light in a life of simple devotion, to seek that intimacy with God that will open our blind eyes to the salvation and glory he promises.

PRAYER

O sing a new song to the Lord,
sing to the Lord all the earth.
O sing to the Lord, bless his name.
Proclaim his help day by day,
tell among the nations his glory
and his wonders among all the peoples.

Psalm 96[95]:1–3)

MEDITATION
Read 1 John 2:3–11

The holy family and
the hidden life
30 DECEMBER

◆◆

*Let the message of Christ, in all its richness, find a home with
you. Teach each other, and advise each other, in all wisdom. With
gratitude in your hearts sing psalms and hymns and inspired
songs to God; and never say or do anything except in the name of
the Lord Jesus, giving thanks to God the Father through him.*

(Colossians 3:16–17)

*Meanwhile the child grew to maturity, and he was filled with
wisdom; and God's favour was with him.*

(Luke 2:40)

After the infancy narratives the Gospels tell us that Joseph and Mary returned
from Egypt and settled in Nazareth. Beyond that there is silence—indeed the
only reported incident during the next thirty years is when Jesus stays behind in
the Temple to listen to and ask questions of the great teachers there. The life of
the holy family is something totally hidden from our view.

Self-evidently they lived and worked normally within their little society. If you
visit Nazareth today you will be shown the town's original well (over which an
orthodox church has been built), which historically was the area's one and only
source of water. For the monument-weary pilgrim it is a refreshing touch of
authenticity! Here, throughout those hidden years, Jesus, Mary and Joseph must
have come to this spot for their water, rubbing shoulders and doubtless passing
the time of day with their neighbours.

Yet beneath that ordinary everyday existence, something extraordinary was
happening. Jesus was being 'filled with wisdom and God's favour' quietly and
unobtrusively. When he first began to preach in his own home-town the reaction
of his fellows to the 'gracious words that came from his lips' (Luke 4:22) was
absolute astonishment. 'But this is Joseph's son, surely?' they all told themselves.
Even as Jesus was experiencing, in human terms, the formative influences of a
normal family life, he was also acquiring the habits of a prayer-life—this we
know from his continuing need, throughout his public ministry, to go off alone
to pray.

One spiritual writer, who truly understood this interior life of prayer, was Paul VI. In 'The Pattern of Nazareth' (an address he gave in 1964) he wrote: 'Here [Nazareth] in this school, one learns why it is necessary to have a spiritual rule of life, if one wishes to follow the teaching of the gospel and become a disciple of Christ... May the silence of Nazareth teach us recollection, inwardness, the disposition to listen to good inspiration and the teaching of true masters. May it teach us the need for, and the value of, preparation, of study and of meditation, of personal inner life of prayer which God alone sees in secret.' Long ago I copied this down as a profound spiritual recipe for those who seriously seek to know God.

In this often frantic life it is the people who have learned the value of silence who can remain calm and untouched by the pressures. Jesus is destined to have a very public life, followed everywhere by huge crowds, and finally in full view of everyone himself being tried, stripped and scourged. Perhaps these thirty years of quiet preparation within his family were what enabled him in the end to cope with three years of so public a ministry.

In our modern world, where family life appears to have disintegrated still further with every new set of statistics, do we not need to re-educate ourselves (and society) on the value of silence and reflection, to gain spiritual nourishment and inner strength? I don't mean in the secular sense of attaining 'self-awareness' or 'self-fulfilment' or any of the other slogans that are bandied about, but in order for us to be an open channel of God's grace to others. If the hidden life of Christ is present among us, that 'pattern of Nazareth' can even today nurture that wisdom which 'deploys her strength from one end of the earth to the other, ordering all things for good' (Wisdom 8:1).

PRAYER

With you is Wisdom, she who knows your works,
she who was present when you made the world;
she understands what is pleasing in your eyes
and what agrees with your commandments.
Despatch her from the holy heavens,
send her forth from your throne of glory
to help me and toil with me
and teach me what is pleasing to you,
since she knows and understands everything.
She will guide me prudently in my undertakings
and will protect me by her glory.

MEDITATION

Compare the rest of Wisdom 9 with the promise
of the Holy Spirit in John 16:5–15

Anointed in truth

◆◆

Children, these are the last days;
you were told that an Antichrist must come,
and now several antichrists have already appeared;
we know from this that these are the last days.
Those rivals of Christ came out of our own number,
*   but they had never really belonged;*
if they had belonged, they would have stayed with us;
but they left us, to prove that not one of them
*   ever belonged to us.*
But you have been anointed by the Holy One,
and have all received the knowledge.
It is not because you do not know the truth that I am
*   writing to you*
but rather because you know it already
and know that no lie can come from the truth.

(1 John 2:18–21)

Today—and in the week of the Christmas season that immediately follows—the Church's readings are all taken from the letters of John, an eloquent diet of quite uncompromising teaching. These letters are, after the joy and wonder of the coming of God, a timely reminder of how, once we have accepted the truth, we have to respond in a most positive manner. John wastes no words, his theology is delivered (as they used to say in westerns) 'shooting from the hip'. I was once with a group of people in church when a section of one of John's letters was read particularly powerfully, and I recall everyone present visibly wincing! Anyone with any spiritual illusions about themselves would soon find themselves well tested reading through these three letters. I think I love them precisely because they are *so* strong. As far as John is concerned, anyone who does not profess the truth that 'Jesus Christ is Lord' is anti-Christ. There's no middle-of-the-road dialogue about it. Anyone who opposes the lordship of Christ is a rival. Full stop.

The scripture scholars tell us that the early Church believed that the second coming of Jesus was imminent, and John is here recalling Jesus' answer to his disciples' question 'What will be the sign of your coming?' 'Many will come', he replied, 'using my name and saying, "I am the Christ"'; and a little later on, 'False Christs and false prophets will arise and produce great signs and portents...' (Matthew 24:3–5, 24). Looking around him and seeing many such counterfeits and rivals in his own day, John concluded that 'these are the last days'. It was premature, but the false prophets have persisted through the ages: in our own time we could be said to have a glut of them, bringing in their wake the ruin of young lives, broken homes, brainwashing, programming and de-programming.

Their approach is subtle but their results are undeniably the signs of anti-christ—not least for instance in the destruction of family life. I personally know of one sect that robbed a young mother and two children of their father for a time (thankfully, he came to his senses in due course), by distributing leaflets that purported to use passages of scripture in justification of their 'philosophy'! Next time you are besieged by a doorstep cult-salesman your Christian response should be to apply the acid test for believers as outlined by John himself: 'It is not every spirit, my dear people, that you can trust; test them to see if they come from God; there are many false prophets, now, in the world. You can tell the spirits that come from God by this: every spirit which acknowledges that Jesus the Christ has come in the flesh is from God; but any spirit which will not say this of Jesus is not from God' (1 John 4:1–3).

Today we pray for John's kind of clarity in our own belief, that we who have been anointed with the Holy Spirit and have received knowledge of the truth, will be able to reflect this truth in our lives and give witness to others who seek the truth.

PRAYER

Indeed you love truth in the heart;
then in the secret of my heart teach me wisdom...
A pure heart create for me, O God,
put a steadfast spirit within me.
Do not cast me away from your presence,
nor deprive me of your holy spirit.

(Psalm 51[50]:6, 10–11)

MEDITATION
Begin to study the First Letter of John

Mother of God 1 JANUARY

◆◆

When the appointed time came, God sent his Son, born of a woman, born a subject of the Law, to redeem the subjects of the Law and to enable us to be adopted as sons. The proof that you are sons is that God has sent the Spirit of his Son into our hearts: the Spirit that cries, 'Abba, Father', and it is this that makes you a son, you are not a slave any more; and if God has made you son, then he has made you heir.

(Galatians 4:4–7)

One of the revelations to be encountered in our search of scripture is how what is being communicated by sign and symbol in the Old Testament provides a preface to, and becomes a reality in, the New Testament. In particular this is true of Mary, who today ('the eighth day') names her child 'Jesus'—the name given by the angel before his conception.

In the Old Testament God's relationship with his people is often likened to the relationship between husband and wife. The prophet Hosea is one who gives us this imagery: the husband will lure his wife away from her infidelity, she will be purified of her sinfulness, and restored to happy union with God. Traditionally in Israel the success of a marriage depended on its fruitfulness, and at the end of his book Hosea describes Israel as an evergreen cypress tree, that is to say a symbol of life, eternally fruitful. Thus is Israel transformed by God from a virgin bride into an eternally fruitful mother.

In the New Testament Mary, virgin daughter of Zion, becomes the living realisation of what before had been sign and symbol: she is to become mother of a new creation, whose firstborn is Jesus, son of Mary, Son of God. We too can share in this family relationship for (as St Paul explains above) through her son's death and resurrection the world receives the Holy Spirit, who comes to dwell in our hearts. This makes us adopted sons and daughters of God. ('All those who believe in the name of [Jesus]' says the prologue to John's Gospel, are given 'power to become children of God'; v. 12.) Thus Mary is not just mother of God, but also mother of all the children of God.

It is my personal belief that just as God entrusted to Mary the responsibility for and care of Jesus—who in his human form needed the love and protection of a normal human upbringing, as we all do—so he entrusted to her the care of his disciples. 'This is your mother' Christ himself said to John (John 19:27), and we today would strive to be his disciples and therefore still in her care. (When we say in the Creed we believe in the communion of saints, we mean we are in communion with all God's Church, past and present.) We have already mentioned that Mary was the first Christian, by receiving Christ through the power of the Holy Spirit. In obedience to the word she was both Christ-bearer and Christ-giver and, if we invite her to, Mary can teach *us* how to give birth to Christ in the world. The motherhood of Israel is perpetuated through Mary and the motherhood of the Church; the evergreen tree continues to give forth fruitfulness; Jesus is still being born in the hearts of men.

There is a vision in the Book of Revelation of the devil waging war, not only on the woman and her male child, but also on the *rest* of her children who bear witness for Jesus. Here is the source of our sad divisions, and what we must pray for today is unity among God's children, so that we may be one as Jesus is one with the Father; and let us ask Mary the mother of Christ to pray with us for that prayer to be answered.

PRAYER

May the Lord bless you from Sion
all the days of your life!
May you see your children's children
in a happy Jerusalem!

(Psalm 128[127]:5–6)

MEDITATION
Read Revelation 12:1–17

Live in Christ

◆◆

> *Keep alive in yourselves what you were taught in*
> *   the beginning:*
> * as long as what you were taught in the beginning is*
> *   alive in you,*
> *you will live in the Son*
> *and in the Father;*
> *and what is promised to you by his own promise*
> *is eternal life...*
> *Live in Christ, then, my children,*
> *so that if he appears, we may have full confidence,*
> *and not turn from him in shame.*
>
> *(1 John 2:24–25, 28)*

In his letter John refers to—though he does not dwell on it for long—the 'end times'. His much more crucial theme is that of keeping the Christian teaching alive, continuing to live in Christ here and now. We too still hear a steady flow of prophetic voices warning us of the end times, and our response must still correspond with John's. The question is, where do I stand? Thérèse of Lisieux warned, 'We only have this life to love him of our own free will': a disturbing thought when you analyse it, for who of us has in fact loved him at anything approaching our capacity? The great commandment (Mark 12:30) was that we should love him totally, 'with all our heart, mind and strength'.

Jesus has told us precisely how to keep our love alive: 'If anyone loves me he will keep my word, and my Father will love him, and we shall come to him and make our home with him'. The promise, you'll note, is open to *anyone*. Sometimes (and I speak for myself here as well) we misunderstand sanctity: we imagine that holy people are born holy and that they have a special gift for keeping love alive. It simply isn't true. God stands at everyone's door knocking, as it says in Revelation. 'If anyone hears my voice and opens... I will come in' (3:20).

What we are actually asked to do is to be forthcoming enough to *allow* the Spirit of God to dwell in us—in our heart—and there gently and silently to make his presence felt. There he can inspire us and re-shape us more and more into the image of himself, all the time building up our capacity to love. It is a process described beautifully by St John of the Cross in his poem, *The Living Flame of Love*:

> *How gently and lovingly you awake in my heart*
> *where you dwell secretly and alone!*
> *And in your sweet breathing,*
> *full of blessing and glory,*
> *how delicately you inspire my love!*

St John of the Cross—whose writings on prayer have greatly influenced the Church over the years—was a living example of the theme of his own book: all his teachings were centred entirely on the word of God in scripture. Scripture is the food of prayer, and prayer is the opening up of ourselves to God, to allow him to dwell in us ('A child of God listens to the words of God' John 8:47). So if we are to keep alive the teachings we have received, our priority must be to continually feed on the word of God in scripture and let it become 'active' within us. Like Mary we must learn to ponder and reflect on what we hear, then allow him to inspire us to give and receive his love until, as St Paul said, 'I live not with my own life but with the life of Christ who lives in me' (Galatians 2:20).

PRAYER

> *My soul, give thanks to the Lord,*
> *all my being, bless his holy name.*
> *My soul, give thanks to the Lord*
> *and never forget all his blessings.*
> *It is he who forgives all your guilt,*
> *who heals every one of your ills,*
> *who redeems your life from the grave,*
> *who crowns you with love and compassion,*
> *who fills your life with good things,*
> *renewing your youth like an eagle's.*

(Psalm 103[102]:1–5)

MEDITATION
Continue your study of the First Letter of John

As pure as Christ
◆◆◆

You know that God is righteous—
then you must recognise that everyone whose life
is righteous
has been begotten by him.
Think of the love that the Father has lavished on us,
by letting us be called God's children;
and that is what we are.
Because the world refused to acknowledge him,
therefore it does not acknowledge us.
My dear people, we are already the children of God
but what we are to be in the future has not yet been revealed;
all we know is, that when it is revealed
we shall be like him
because we shall see him as he really is.
Surely everyone who entertains this hope
must purify himself, must try to be as pure as Christ.
Anyone who sins at all
breaks the law,
because to sin is to break the law.
Now you know that he appeared in order to
abolish sin,
and that in him there is no sin;
anyone who lives in God does not sin,
and anyone who sins
has never seen him or known him.

(1 John 2:29–3:6)

Once again John's letter doesn't pull any punches. Anyone, he is saying, who claims to be living in union with God must be expressing this in the kind of life he leads. Since he allows us to be called his children, we have an obligation in return to honour him as all children should honour their parents—that is, by trying to lead a righteous life.

So far so good, but in order to lead a righteous life, John tells us, we must be willing to be purified. Now it can scarcely be said that purification is one of the most popular themes of the Bible: it tends to be regarded either as an abstraction or else as a kind of ritual procedure. Yet if we are seriously seeking God, one of the signs of our authenticity is that we will gradually come to *desire* purification. 'Who shall climb the mountain of the Lord? Who shall stand in his holy place?' asks the psalmist (24[23]:3). Comes the answer: 'The man with clean hands and pure heart.' Jesus is even more explicit when he says that it is the pure in heart who actually see God (Matthew 5:8). It is, therefore, a state in which those genuinely seeking God would naturally wish to be.

It seems to me that purification is not just something we can set about doing. Of course it requires an act of will—we have (as St Paul says) to work for our salvation (Philippians 2:12). But it also requires the right pre-disposition on our part. We need to allow God to 'enlighten the eyes of our mind', in the words of Ephesians 3. This he will do not with the pointed finger of accusation, but with a gentleness that both illuminates the problem, and the way out of it. If I'm self-centred it's because... If I'm possessive it's because... Sometimes our problems may not even be our own fault, and the realisation of that in itself can be a liberating experience. Of course it *is* painful sometimes to face up to reality: the devious heart that Jeremiah spoke of (17:9) can so easily be caught up in a web of self-deception, avoiding the pain but evading the problem as well. If a growth is going to kill you, you simply have to say 'yes' to the surgeon and trust in his skill. God in his infinite patience will always wait for our eventual 'yes', however hesitant.

We therefore must learn to *trust* God, as the people of Israel learned to trust him through the testing-time of the exodus. As for them, so for us the ultimate promise is that of freedom and a sense of peace. The peace that passes all understanding is that which, in the midst of trials and conflict, is able to trust God totally. And (as we have seen) what better example of this is there than St Stephen who, even as he was being stoned to death, was able to say, 'Lord Jesus, receive my spirit and do not hold this against them'?

Certainly we may find that kind of trust a long, long way ahead of us. But we are not alone, as St Paul pointed out: 'I am no longer trying for perfection by my own efforts, the perfection that comes from the Law, but I want only the perfection that comes through faith in Christ, and is from God and based on faith... Not that I have become perfect yet: I have not yet won, but I am still running, trying to capture the prize for which Christ Jesus captured me' (Philippians 3:9, 12).

PRAYER

A pure heart create for me, O God,
put a steadfast spirit within me.
Do not cast me away from your presence,
nor deprive me of your holy spirit.

(Psalm 51[50]:10–11)

MEDITATION

Continue your study of the First Letter of John

Be holy

◆◆◆

My children, do not let anyone lead you astray:
to live a holy life
is to be holy just as [God] is holy;
to lead a sinful life is to belong to the devil,
since the devil was a sinner from the beginning.
It was to undo all that the devil has done
that the Son of God appeared.
No one who has been begotten by God sins;
because God's seed remains inside him,
he cannot sin when he has been begotten by God.
In this way we distinguish the children of God
from the children of the devil:
anybody not living a holy life
and not loving his brother
is no child of God's.

(1 John 3:7–10)

Here, as ever, John challenges us to set our individual sights high: we must live a holy life. He is penetratingly direct—we either belong to God or to the devil, there are no grey areas. It is as unequivocal a message as Jesus' original teaching (compare John 8), and a positive restatement of the alternatives outlined all through the Bible: life or death, blessing or curse, good or evil, God or the devil. John's letter emphasises that we are the children of God, his heirs: therefore we must be like God, we must turn aside from sin, be made holy. The choice is clear.

We live today, however, in an age of compromise, when anything seems to go and when Christian values have largely been shrugged aside as irrelevant to modern requirements. Even within the churches the gospel message gets a sugar coating, its challenge muted. Society has been 'led astray' and we can observe violence and crime on the increase, family life disintegrating with so many marriages ending in divorce and thousands of our children growing up insecure. We see pornography openly displayed in high streets, children having access to macabre and sick videos. Bookshops even give shelf-space to studies of the occult and satanism, which (and this is one of the most alarming facets of our secularised society) itself gains momentum. In June 1972 *Time* magazine observed: 'Recent history has shown terrifyingly enough, that the demonic lies barely beneath the surface, ready to catch men unawares with new and more horrible manifestations...', words which are perhaps even more relevant today, over thirty years later.

All this makes the call to holiness an ever more urgent one, for 'it was to undo all that the devil has done that God's Son appeared'. We have already remarked in this book how one human life united with God can undo immeasurable damage caused by the enemy, and John underlines the very point: 'Anyone who has been begotten by God has already overcome the world; this is the victory over the world—our faith' (5:4). By our baptism in Christ—through having received the Holy Spirit—God's seed remains in us. It is up to us to choose whether or not to surrender our lives to this indwelling of God, to throw off the sin that hinders us but clings so easily, to persevere in faith. (Hebrews 10:19 to the end of chapter 12 is a wonderful instruction on a persevering faith, by the way.) The call to be holy in a world shrouded in unbelief is a serious, vital challenge. True holiness is a life surrendered to God in prayer and loving: it is learning to die to self in order to rise to life. 'I tell you, most solemnly, unless a wheat grain falls on the ground and dies, it remains only a single grain; but if it dies, it yields a rich harvest' (John 12:24).

PRAYER

They are happy, whose strength is in you,
in whose hearts are the roads to Sion.
As they go through the Bitter Valley
they make it a place of springs,
the autumn rain covers it with blessings.
They walk with ever growing strength,
they will see the God of gods in Sion.

(Psalm 84[83]:5–7)

MEDITATION

Continue your study of the First Letter of John

This has taught us love   5 JANUARY

◆◆◆

This has taught us love—
that he gave up his life for us;
and we, too, ought to give up our lives for our brothers.
If a man who was rich enough in this world's goods
saw that one of his brothers was in need,
but closed his heart to him,
how could the love of God be living in him?
My children,
our love is not to be just words or mere talk,
but something real and active;
only by this can we be certain
that we are children of the truth
and be able to quieten our conscience in his presence,
whatever accusations it may raise against us,
because God is greater than our conscience and
he knows everything.
My dear people,
if we cannot be condemned by our own conscience,
we need not be afraid in God's presence.

(1 John 3:16–21)

Today the Christmas season of celebration comes to an end. Throughout this book we have read about and reflected on the historical events that preceded the birth of Christ, and we have commemorated the feast itself. It is in quiet reflection on the mysteries of God's coming (on his passion and death and resurrection, as well as his birth) that faith is born in us—but something else must happen within us, even as we feast on the wonder of God—and that is: we must *respond*. We can spend a lifetime gazing at a pearl of great price in a shop window, or we can sell all we have and possess it. Jesus' words to the woman at the well, 'If only you knew what God is offering!' are his words to us too. As we now stand before God incarnate, we too can respond like her and simply say, 'Give me some' (John 4:10, 15).

What God is offering is an intimate relationship, and it's from that relationship we can learn the nature of love, our pattern and paragon of love (as

John says above) being the life of Jesus. For 'God loved the world so much that he gave his only Son, so that everyone who believes in him... may have eternal life' (John 3:16). As Jesus gave up his life for us, so our response is to give our lives to God—that is love. It involves the sacrifice of 'self' so that he can 'grow greater and I grow smaller' (John 3:30) and the fruits of love (turning the other cheek, praying for those who persecute me, being a cheerful giver, and so on) can proceed from the heart. We cannot love with flexed muscles and gritted teeth: pure love has to be motivated by a loving heart.

Entrance, as it were, to the Holy Spirit's school of loving is through prayer. In prayer we learn to receive the love of God and to reciprocate it, and through his love we will learn to love ourselves. Once that has happened we will be free to love others in a selfless way, and be living witnesses to those other Christian virtues which spring from love: 'joy, peace, patience, kindness, goodness, trustfulness, gentleness, self-control' (Galatians 5:22–23). Yet again I am drawn to one of the thoughts of Thérèse of Lisieux: in the end we will not be judged according to how much we have sinned, but how much we have loved.

To sum up very briefly on this final day of the season: our response to the birth of Jesus should be our own rebirth, a renewal of our personal relationship with God whose promise (through the prophet Ezekiel) was that he would remove our hearts of stone and give us a heart of flesh (11:19). A heart given to God is a heart given to love. 'Let us love one another since love comes from God, and everyone who loves is begotten by God and knows God. Anyone who fails to love can never have known God, because *God is love*' (1 John 4:7–8).

PRAYER FOR EVERY DAY OF THE YEAR

Come, Holy Spirit,
fill the hearts of your faithful.
Enkindle in them the fire of your love.
Send forth your spirit
and they shall be created
and you shall renew the face of the earth.
Amen

MEDITATION
Continue (and finish) your study of the First
Letter of John

Epiphany   6 JANUARY
◆◆

Arise, shine out, for your light has come,
the glory of the Lord is rising on you,
though night still covers the earth
and darkness the peoples.
Above you the Lord now rises
and above you his glory appears.
The nations come to your light
and kings to your dawning brightness.
Lift up your eyes and look round:
all are assembling and coming towards you,
your sons from far away
and your daughters being tenderly carried.
At this sight you will grow radiant,
your heart throbbing and full;
since the riches of the sea will flow to you,
the wealth of the nations come to you;
Camels in throngs will cover you,
and dromedaries of Midian and Ephah;
everyone in Sheba will come,
bringing gold and incense
and singing the praise of the Lord.

(Isaiah 60:1–6)

We celebrate today the feast of Christ's appearance in the world, his epiphany. A new light shone out in the darkness then, and now that light is firmly established in heaven, perpetually shining, unquenchable. Anyone on earth who sets out on a journey in search of God will be led by this light: eventually all the pilgrim people of the world will be brought to Bethlehem and the child in the manger. No matter what their status, background or colour—the Communist with no Bible, the Amazon Indian unaware of the rest of civilisation, all the unbaptized who have never heard the name Jesus—the light shines for every man who walks in darkness.

There are many routes to God, but only one light. The wise men and the shepherds found their way to the stable by quite different paths but by following the same star. The shepherds, poor and simple, but sons of Israel reared on the scriptures, quite spontaneously accepted the message of the angel. Not for them the grappling with the complexities of science or the intellect: theirs is a journey of simplicity and child-like faith. In contrast the wise men, Gentiles with no religious upbringing, stumbled on the same truth by a process of reasoning and through their knowledge of the world. They were open-minded enough to embark on the journey—they came to Bethlehem in a spirit of enquiry.

They also came bearing gifts, strange gifts, but Fr Geoffrey Preston has a most thoughtful reflection on their significance in his commentary on Epiphany in his book *Hallowing the Time**. They represent, he suggests, all the questions posed by a non-believing world: gold, the currency of politics, economics and commerce; frankincense, the material of worship, signifies man's questions about the divine; and myrrh, the ointment of death, 'the supreme question mark set against all the activities of man'. Thus all man's searching is laid at the manger, wherein lies the answer, the 'way, the truth and the life'.

As we look forward at this Epiphany to the greater Epiphany that is yet to come, I would like to leave you with a most beautiful passage from Fr Preston's book:

'With the wise men we celebrate the supreme epiphany of the glory of our great God and of our saviour Jesus Christ, that is, his appearing in glory at the end of time. Love for that appearing is meant to permeate our love for all the preliminary epiphanies; and we love them aright when our delight in them does not dilute our longing for the last and greatest epiphany. We are given the eucharistic bread and the bread of the Word as food for our pilgrimage, rations for the way. We are given the wine of the eucharist and the wine of song and psalm to cheer our hearts in this our exile. But they are intended to make us more hungry and more thirsty for what we still have only in promise and foreshadowing. Blessed, happy, fortunate are those who hunger and thirst like this, who still crave for God's great epiphany even though they have already been filled with good things. Happy are they, says the Lord himself, because they will have their fill.'

* *Darton, Longman and Todd (Paulist Press), 1980.*

PRAYER FOR EVERY EVENING OF THE YEAR

Now, master, you can let your servant go in peace,
just as you promised;
because my eyes have seen the salvation
which you have prepared for all the nations to see,
a light to enlighten the pagans
and the glory of your people Israel.

(Luke 2:29–32)

MEDITATION
Read Matthew 2:1–12

Also by Delia Smith

A Feast for Lent

REFLECTIONS ON EASTER FOR EVERY DAY IN LENT

A Feast for Lent was first published by BRF in 1983. It was an immediate bestseller and has continued to delight thousands of readers year after year. Many have written to say that they now couldn't imagine preparing for Easter without Delia Smith and the readings and reflections she shares in *A Feast for Lent*.

'Delia Smith is writing about her own voyage of discovery. Her choice of readings (and the sharing of her thoughts and prayers as she reads) takes us through the steps of conversion—that change of heart and mind that must begin with the recognition of our own weakness and reach out for peace in the compassion and kindness of God.

'This is a helpful and hopeful book, where the Word of God steps out of the past to become a personal and moving experience in everyday life. It is an experience we could all come to share more deeply this Lent' (from the foreword by Bishop Victor Guazzelli).

ISBN 978 0 7459 3256 9   £6.99
Available from your local Christian bookshop or, in case of difficulty, direct from BRF using the order form opposite.

ORDER FORM

Ref	Title	Price	Qty	Total
3256 9	A Feast for Lent	£6.99		

POSTAGE AND PACKING CHARGES					Postage and packing:	
Order value	UK	Europe	Surface	Air Mail	Donation:	
£7.00 & under	£1.25	£3.00	£3.50	£5.50	**Total enclosed:**	
£7.01–£30.00	£2.25	£5.50	£6.50	£10.00		
Over £30.00	free	prices on request				

Name _____ Account Number _____

Address_____

_____ Postcode _____

Telephone Number _____ Email _____

Payment by: ☐ Cheque ☐ Mastercard ☐ Visa ☐ Postal Order ☐ Maestro

Card no. ☐☐☐☐ ☐☐☐☐ ☐☐☐☐ ☐☐☐☐

Expires ☐☐ ☐☐ Security code ☐☐☐ Issue no. ☐☐☐

Signature _____ Date _____

All orders must be accompanied by the appropriate payment.

Please send your completed order form to:
BRF, First Floor, Elsfield Hall, 15–17 Elsfield Way, Oxford OX2 8FG
Tel. 01865 319700 / Fax. 01865 319701 Email: enquiries@brf.org.uk

☐ Please send me further information about BRF publications.

Available from your local Christian bookshop.   BRF is a Registered Charity

brf

Resourcing your spiritual journey

through...

- Bible reading notes
- Books for Advent & Lent
- Books for Bible study and prayer
- Books to resource those working with under 11s in school, church and at home

- Quiet days and retreats
- Training for primary teachers and children's leaders
- Godly Play
- Barnabas RE Days

For more information, visit the **brf** website at **www.brf.org.uk**